Among Canyon Shadows

An Eastern Artist in Western Colorado

Among Canyon Shadows

An Eastern Artist in Western Colorado

Joyce B. Lohse

Filter Press, LLC

Filter Press, LLC
Westcliffe, Colorado
www.FilterPressBooks.com
719-481-2420

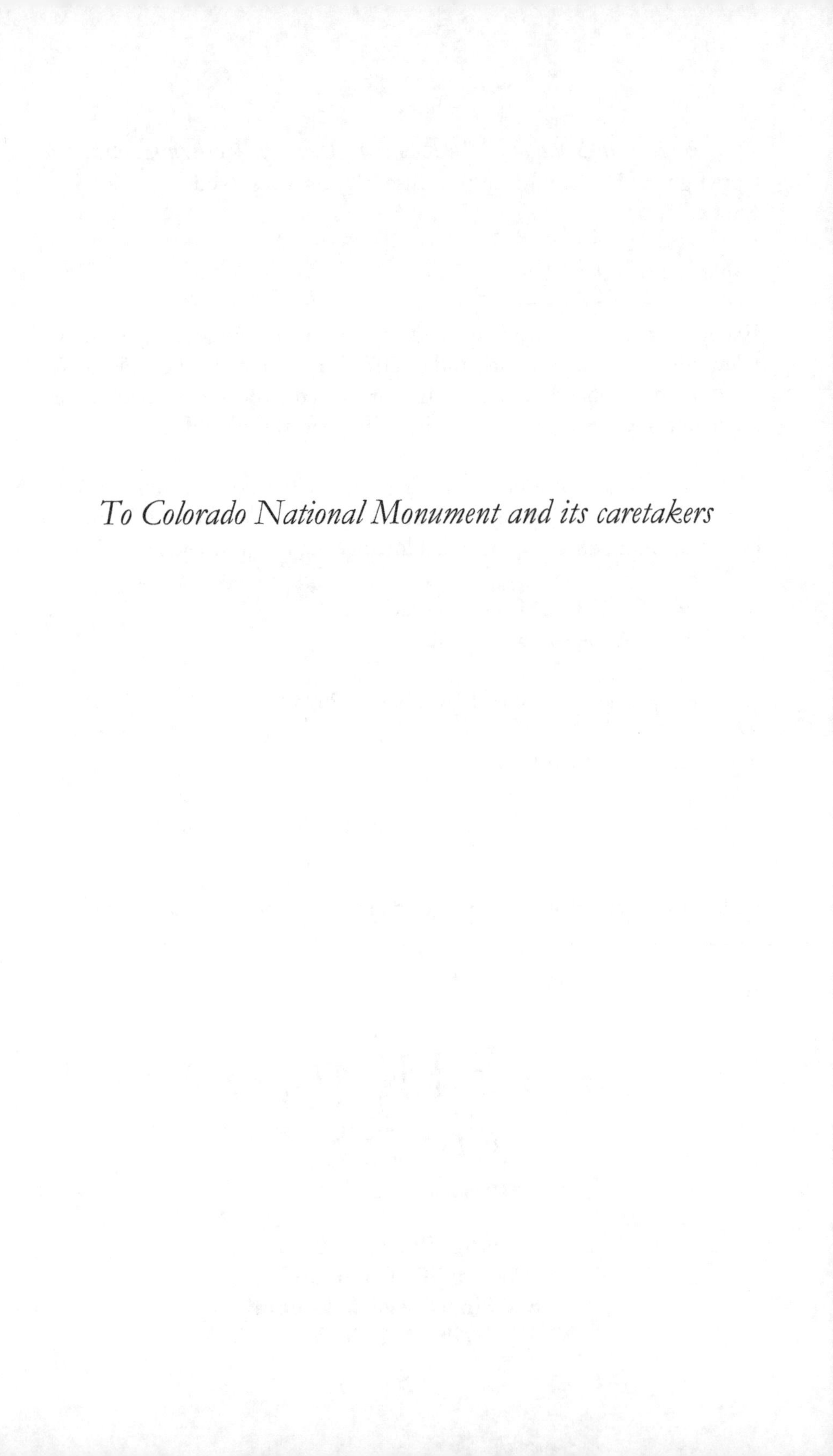

To Colorado National Monument and its caretakers

Contents

Preface

As sometimes happens, I was not looking for a story when a man on a horse caught my attention. I knew a little bit about John Otto. He was the eccentric trail builder who was responsible for the establishment of Colorado National Monument, a thirty-two-square-mile parcel of scenery filled with colorful canyons and rock formations near Grand Junction, Colorado. After several visits to the monument park, my interest in local history increased. I wanted to learn more about the fellow on the horse displayed on a bronze plaque at the park's visitor center.

At Lithic Bookstore in Fruita, Colorado, a used book entitled *John Otto of Colorado National Monument* fell into my hands. It was signed, "Boostingly Yours" by author Alan J. Kania. The next page caught my attention. The book dedication read, "To

**Bronze plaque of John Otto at the
Colorado National Monument Visitor Center.**

Beatrice Farnham—Whatever happened to you?"

A message of that sort usually grabs me in cemeteries. As a multi-published biographer, this question was an arrow aimed straight at my journalist heart. I bought the book. How hard could it be to learn whatever happened to Beatrice Farnham? I could research her life while reading about John Otto. Who was she? Where did she come from? Where did she go—and why? I was hooked.

The Mesa County Public Library offered vital assistance from the beginning. The programs they hosted with the Mesa County Historical Society were priceless. Park rangers at Colorado National Monument were especially helpful and encouraging, as was the Colorado National Monument Association.

While we were cooped up indoors during the COVID epidemic, I did plenty of research about many subjects online, always slipping some time in for Beatrice Farnham. I was fortunate to receive help from history museums in Patrick County, Virginia and in Paso Robles, California. They were both generous with information.

My growing interest in John Otto and Beatrice Farnham coincided with the restoration of Grand Junction's historic train station, planned and managed by the Friends of Grand Junction Union Depot. During an open house, I joined the organization and then rested on a polished wooden passenger bench. Surrounded by the fine old building's interior with light streaming through dim leaded glass, I slipped back in history and wondered if Beatrice had sat where I was sitting while she waited for the train back to Boston in 1911. What was she thinking? How did she feel? Did she plan to return?

Little evidence of Beatrice Farnham's artistic activity in the Grand Valley remains. Her landscape sketches and paintings are absent. Her Native American-style designs were applied to

Beatrice Farnham dressed in western clothing, rides
in Colorado National Monument. Image published in *Collier's:
The National Weekly*, July 1, 1911.

home décor, which was sold commercially. If she produced fine
artworks, she retained them or they were sold to private collec-
tors. It is unknown whether she returned back east with art to
sell as she intended.

Beatrice's lasting artistic statement was her wardrobe. Her
woven poncho, western-style hat, boots, saddlebag, and split

riding skirt caused quite a stir and caught attention. She was effusive when she discussed riding astride across the open plains and often posed to be photographed in her attire. Photos of Beatrice in her western outfit are her most lasting artistic statement.

I took advantage of guided hikes and art classes with the Colorado National Monument Association to get a feel for drawing and painting outdoors. High desert terrain was new and enchanting to me. I hiked on paths Beatrice had either walked or ridden on horseback among canyon shadows. Colorado National Monument was a scenic, wild wonderland.

As with my other biographical subjects, I retrieved quotations, to allow Beatrice Farnham's voice to be heard and to become a part of her story. I hope readers enjoy sharing Beatrice's trail during her time spent in western Colorado and beyond, and during her partnership with an intrepid, quirky trail guide named John Otto.

Happy trails,
Joyce B. Lohse
April 18, 2026

Readers Review *Among Canyon Shadows*

In *Among Canyon Shadows*, Joyce Lohse vividly brings Colorado's history to life through the perspectives of trail builder John Otto and artist Beatrice Farnham. The Colorado National Monument unfolds with its rugged terrain, interwoven with themes of romance and heartbreak. Lohse enriches their journey with Farnham's profound appreciation for the art and lifestyle of southwest Indigenous Peoples. Through her narrative, she paints a compelling portrait of bravery, independence, and free-spiritedness.

Carmen Peone – Award-winning Author of
Broken Bondage (Seven Tine Ranch series)

~ ~ ~ ~ ~

This is an intriguing story of two people of independent spirit whose lives crossed in the rugged splendor of Colorado National Monument. The human element, the historical detail, and the realistic treatment will hold the reader's interest.

John D. Nesbitt – Wyoming writer, college educator,
and multi award-winning western author

PART 1

*Each spring the fever for the open plains and long rides
in the shadows of mountains possesses me and I
drop everything, then after six or seven weeks I go back
with renewed zeal and a head full of ideas to my work.*
Beatrice Farnham
Albuquerque Morning Journal, **January 27, 1911**

CHAPTER 1

A Western "Howdy"

On a January morning in 1911, a chilly breeze blew across the train platform in Albuquerque, New Mexico. A woman dressed in western attire walked with a confident stride toward the depot. Although it was cloudy, her firmly placed broad-brimmed hat was tilted forward to shade her face as she strode from the Alvarado Hotel to the adjoining train station. The famous hotel was operated by the Atchison, Topeka and Santa Fe Railroad in conjunction with Fred Harvey's restaurants, which were well-known for hospitality in the West.

The woman's long skirt pressed against her legs as she walked on toward the Indian Building adjacent to the train station. A few pedestrians turned slightly to catch a glimpse as she passed by. Some stared without compunction.

Her pace slowed as she approached displays of handcrafted Native American merchandise for sale, which she observed with interest. She was eager to study more Native art and designs before the train transported her to remote pueblos west of Albuquerque.

The Santa Fe Railroad Station and Native American art sellers, Albuquerque, New Mexico. Postcard circa 1910.

Tribe members from the Isleta Pueblo and Santo Domingo Pueblo exhibited pottery and jewelry on rugs and blankets along the path. While they awaited their train's departure, travelers could browse among additional crafts and merchandise inside the Indian Building.

The morning after her departure, on January 27, 1911, *The Albuquerque Morning Journal* reported noteworthy sightings in its column "Celebrities Pass Through." The attractive eastern artist had been noticed and interviewed:

Yesterday when a tall, striking woman gowned in a mixture [of] cowboy and Indian attire appeared at the Santa Fe station the few people who loitered around, paused to stare and conjecture. . . . The woman who was the object of curiosity and comment is—Beatrice Farnham, noted artist, who has figured on the pages of the *New York World, Colliers'* and many other well-known press organs.

Beatrice, an accomplished artist from South Weymouth, Massachusetts, relished her solo travels on west-bound cross-country trains. Once a year, she visited New Mexico to collect artwork and study designs among Native American artisans and local tribes. This trip to New Mexico was earlier than usual and would coincide with her thirty-fifth birthday the following week on February 5, 1911.

Beatrice was no stranger to New Mexico and was dressed for the cold, high country desert in January. She wore a brightly colored serape, a blanket-like garment made of hand-woven wool that provided warmth, along with a pair of fringed leather gloves. The serape covered her white blouse, which she wore with a split dark twill skirt crafted using her own design to allow her to ride astride on horseback.

Her attraction to New Mexico had begun a decade earlier when she learned about Indigenous cultures at San Francisco's

The Indian Building , Albuquerque, New Mexico.
Postcard circa 1906.

Hopkins Art Institute. Her studies led her to create artwork with a focus on southwestern art and design.

After admiring the merchandise, Beatrice walked across the brick-paved train platform, her loud footsteps in western boots announcing her progress. A large leather pouch decorated with tribal beadwork, slung across her shoulder, bulged with her belongings. A riding quirt made of braided leather and colorful dyed horsehair hung from a woven sash at her waist and swayed with each step. The eastern artist, whose eye-catching attire and deeply tanned complexion was a novelty in the East, blended in with Native people in the Southwest.

But her aggressive stride and flamboyant style also invited attention in New Mexico. Travelers visiting this remote western area typically dressed in tailored suits made in tones of gray, brown, and black in contrast to her bright southwestern designs and assertive demeanor. Her clothing, which appeared eccentric or strange to some people, suited her purpose, which was to immerse herself in the culture and landscape of the Southwest.

Let them stare.

Beatrice's passion for adventure began when she was a teenager, when her family moved from Maine to Paso Robles, California in 1891. The long train ride, across the entire continent, allowed the adventurous fifteen-year-old to see the expanse of the United States. The move kindled her curiosity and her desire to explore the nation's mountains, deserts, and wide-open prairies.

After Beatrice graduated from Paso Robles High School in June 1896, she attended art school in San Francisco. When she returned to the East Coast, she lived with her family in South Weymouth, Massachusetts, a town located close to Boston. She promoted her artwork on the East Coast and found inspiration in the Southwest, which was accessible by passenger railroad.

Compared to her home on the East Coast, New Mexico's

winter sunshine, cool dry air, friendly people, and slower pace appealed to Beatrice. Automobile traffic was still a rarity, especially on trails connecting scattered towns and settlements. She loved nothing more than to ride a good cowpony across open range, surrounded by distant mountains and mesas.

While Beatrice indulged her love of western landscape and adventure, her trips also allowed her to bring western art and designs back to clients in the East. Interest in southwestern art was thriving, and business was good. Her travels to New Mexico immersed her in the source of her inspiration and to acquire new ideas and materials for artwork and home decor, which she sold to individuals, merchants, and agents on the East Coast.

On that day in January 1911, when Beatrice waited for her train and was interviewed by the *Morning Journal* reporter, she was cordial, candid, forthcoming, and arrogant. At times like this, she relished news attention and was happy to give her opinions:

Yes, I attribute my success solely to my knowledge of the Indian's craftsmanship and habits of life—to that and my grit. You know they say everyone has to commence at the bottom of the ladder and climb up, but I have a different idea. I believe in getting to the top first and taking in the details later. There is more chance of a grub stake that way.

Regarding her New Mexico visits, the newspaper quoted Beatrice as saying:

I have lived in New York five years and have never gotten over being homesick. Each spring the fever for the open plains and long rides in the shadows of mountains possesses me and I drop everything, then after six or seven weeks I go back with renewed zeal and a head full of ideas to my work.. . . "Do I like the west? I love it—it's my first love, for I was raised in California."

Later, on February 26, 1911, she elaborated on her love of the West in *The St. Louis Post-Dispatch*:

You get a breadth of view in the big open spaces, and it is mental as well as physical. You get a perspective of yourself. You see just how small you are—and maybe it's the bracing air, for health is the greatest inspiration after all. But something fires you with ambition to come back and beat the world.

Beatrice was exuberant about a recent horseback ride along the base of the Sandia Mountains in New Mexico. Exhilarated by her ride, she told the reporter, "I had a glorious day and stored a bunch of ideas from the mesa and mountains." She was eager to apply her impressions in her artwork.

Her designs for accent pieces were especially popular with her clients. Stenciled Native American figures were painted on fine woven fabric to create accent pillows. Leather fringe trim and bits of aromatic cedar, juniper, and pine needles in the pillow filling resulted in a unique southwestern decoration.

After her perusal of artisan displays in Albuquerque, Beatrice watched weavers and spinners at their crafts. Finally, she returned to the train station and boarded a westbound train for a forty-five-mile ride to the Laguna Reservation Pueblo and Mission.

When she left the train at the Laguna station, she could see the steep, winding dirt road leading up to Acoma Pueblo and San Estevan del Rey Mission Church. The pueblo was located atop a sandstone mesa more than 350 feet tall. The remote settlement was more than two thousand years old. Local artisans continued to preserve their self-reliant community, culture, history, and traditions through the creation of distinctive art and pottery.

Artwork was not Beatrice's only interest. While women back east were crusading for suffrage, she was developing insights about independent living based on the matriarchal cultures of local tribes. In her opinion, citified young females stuck in stifling and unhealthy lifestyles would benefit from outdoor living and by learning skills to become independent. If she could bring eastern ladies out west, she could teach them to live outdoors in harmony with nature. Ideas were percolating and her plans were developing.

A few weeks later, on her return train journey from Albuquerque to Boston, Beatrice created a stir in St. Louis. She stopped there for an overnight stay at the upscale Planters Hotel and was interviewed by popular *St. Louis Post-Dispatch* journalist and illustrator, Marguerite Martyn. Guests and staff at the swank lodging were stunned by the appearance of the eastern artist wearing western attire in the lively city. She could hardly ignore the

A *St. Louis Post-Dispatch* illustration by Marguerite Martyn shows Beatrice observing a lady and her dog at the Planters Hotel, February 26, 1911.

stares and rude remarks. She was called a "barbarian" in a "freakish costume."

Beatrice moved on to the hotel's Turkish Den adjacent to the lobby to remove herself from comments and stares. She found herself surrounded by exotic decor in dim light. Every nook and cranny boasted brocaded upholstery, woven rugs, painted ceramic tiles, plush fringed pillows, tassels, and gold trim. A heavy scent of smoke lingered in the room, where cigarette, cigar, and pipe tobacco were frequently in use.

Whether by choice or adherence to convention, reporter Marguerite Martyn stepped forward to greet Beatrice and guide her to a more comfortable setting. She escorted Beatrice beyond the lobby with its noisy gawkers and away from the smoky gloom of the Turkish Den. They sat down to chat in a brightly lighted "ladies area" with garden furnishings.

When the journalist and visiting artist were comfortably settled, they conversed about many topics. Fashionable young

The Turkish Den in the Planters Hotel in St. Louis.
Postcard circa 1906.

women strolled by and slowed to observe them. Several lingered and leaned closer to listen with curiosity as the journalist and artist chatted.

The following day, on Sunday, February 26, 1911, the conversation with Beatrice about her western adventures filled the entire front page of *The St. Louis Post-Dispatch*. A large headline stated, THE MORE I SEE OF CIVILIZATION THE MORE I LIKE—INDIANS.

The bold, attention-grabbing headline expressed Beatrice's appreciation of Native American culture. Martyn paraphrased Beatrice's remarks throughout the article. The piece was illustrated with drawings that highlighted Beatrice's conspicuous attire. In one sketch, Beatrice appeared tall and lean in her split riding skirt and boots, colorful western jacket, and wide brimmed hat with a jaunty feather stuck in the hatband.

In the interview, Beatrice responded to a question about her immersion in southwestern Native culture and art:

Front page of the February 26, 1911, *St. Louis Post-Dispatch*

When I was in my teens my family backed me into an art school and I stayed there five years, but I get more inspiration, more knowledge of color and composition, more of technique and execution in a day out there on my big playground than I did in all the years of hard labor in the art school.

Apparently, she questioned the value of her traditional art school education and found that her "big playground" on the open range provided all the knowledge and inspiration she required.

With encouragement from the reporter, Beatrice continued, expounding on the virtues of Navajo culture:

Civilization! Why, the Navajos have a civilization that is older and more tried and true than this. It makes ours look pallid and sickly. . . .

"Your D. A. R.'s," she went on, "think they are very old families and all that. Why, I know Indian grandmothers who are able to relate family history and legends that date back to the great flood. . . They have family heirlooms. Beads worn thin as wafers, and pottery of a glaze that only age can reproduce; and old textiles and basketry which no money can buy from them.

"Your suffragettes think they are very advanced. Why, the Navajo women have always had the purse strings and laid down the law to their braves. . . . She owns all the sheep and the products therefrom."

The cluster of stylish young ladies who gathered to listen to her opinions discovered that Beatrice also enjoyed dressing in current styles. She had tried the latest craze, a hobble skirt, which ballooned over the legs and gathered with a tight-fitting hem around both ankles. When she realized the snug fit at her feet impeded walking, she abandoned the garment.

Beatrice preferred to discuss her views about the progressive role of women in business. "You are all alone, you see. You are not influenced and swayed by other minds. You are certain to expand and grow strong and self-reliant and original."

Regarding her latest visit to New Mexico, Beatrice said:

I went out there to find out about Indian basketry, textile weaving and some of the secrets of their potteries, dyes and designs that I could apply to the interior decoration of modern homes. I learned some tricks at first hand that give my work distinction, which I see others trying to imitate and manufacture in factories, in vain.

Beatrice's opinion of Native Americans, from the February 26, 1911, *St. Louis Post-Dispatch*, illustrated by Marguerite Martyn.

Sketch of Beatrice wearing western clothing, from the March 22, 1912, *Los Angeles Times*. In the corner of the sketch, Beatrice is shown drawing a cherub.

The journalist coaxed Beatrice to talk about her forthcoming trip to see a "forest ranger" she had met the previous summer in western Colorado. The man in question was John Otto, a trail builder and guide in an area soon to become a national park or monument. Beatrice had traveled to Colorado in 1910 to explore new vistas and paint landscapes and canyons. She had been guided through the area by Otto and planned to return to Colorado to see more landscapes and to visit her intriguing trail guide.

Her escort, trail builder John Otto, was a rugged, straightforward outdoorsman, who was just her type. Beatrice pulled up her sleeve to show off the gold bracelet she wore. It was inscribed with the western greeting, "Howdy". She identified the giver of the gift by saying, "He is a forest ranger, and a mighty fine pal."

Encouraged by the cluster of bystanders, Beatrice's storytelling was in high gear:

Culture? I know of Indians who are more cultured in the real sense of the word than your so-called polished men of the East. . . . The other day I rode 40 miles with an Indian who caught up with me out on the mesa. He advised me to take a trail he knew of. It was a new one to me, but I did not think of being afraid, and he was as deferential as any knight of the drawing-room all the way. Before we ended the journey five other rangers had joined us and not one of those men presumed upon my friendliness.

In response to the stares and jeers that erupted when she entered the hotel, she said, "All Indians have an inborn sense of courtesy and hospitality toward strangers that would forbid such manners as cultivated strangers have shown me here this morning."

Martyn completed the interview by asking a brash, leading

question: "Why don't you stay out there, if you like it so well?"

Beatrice considered her reply, and stated simply, "Maybe I will someday."

The following day, when Martyn's news article and sketches filled the Sunday morning *St. Louis Post-Dispatch*, Beatrice left St. Louis and continued her railroad journey back to Boston. She was full of ideas to implement and share through her artwork. Newspaper attention bolstered her visibility, recognition, optimism, and ego. Her outlook was bright.

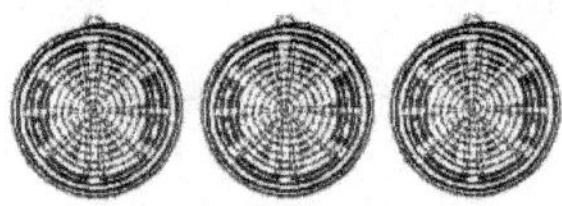

Two months later, Beatrice again traveled on the iron rails across the county. On this trip, she did not plan a route into New Mexico. Instead, she continued winding westward through the twists, turns, and elevated passes over the majestic Rocky Mountains. She looked forward to arriving in western Colorado to say "howdy" to her pal and trail guide, John Otto. After all, he was the intelligent, direct type of man she favored, and "a mighty fine pal." They had corresponded since her visit the previous summer, and he encouraged her to return. As she rode the train across the continent, she had plenty of time to think about the possibilities that awaited her in Colorado's Grand Valley.

CHAPTER 2

An Eastern Artist

Beatrice's love of the outdoors, plants, animals, and the freedom of open space came naturally. She was born in rural Maine, where she lived with her family on her grandparents' farm. As a young child, she explored her environment, learned about nature, cared for livestock, and enjoyed horseback riding. Her mother and grandmother were also close at hand to teach her lessons in propriety and domestic skills.

Flora Beatrice Farnham was born February 5, 1876, one hundred years after the United States of America declared independence. Colorado acquired statehood the year of her birth and became known as the Centennial State. The farm where her parents, Briggs and Minnie Farnham, lived was owned by her grandfather, Ebenezer "Eben" Farnham, and was located near Jefferson in Lincoln County, Maine. Beatrice was the only child in her family.

Beatrice's father, Briggs, managed the farm toward the end of her grandfather's life. When her grandfather died in 1881, Briggs's older brother James, took over management of the farm.

A photo of Beatrice on her horse Pigeon.
St. Louis Post-Dispatch, February 26, 1911.

By 1885, Briggs was postmaster in the nearby town of East Jefferson, Maine. Within five years, the family moved to Pemaquid, also known as Bristol, on the Atlantic coast. There, Briggs ran the Bay View Store and was also town clerk.

Another of Briggs's older brothers, Charles, was a Civil War veteran whose arm had been amputated. Charles and his family (who used the spelling *Farnum* instead of *Farnham*) had migrated to the West Coast. By 1880, Charles worked as a San Francisco merchant and resided in Lompoc in Santa Barbara County. He encouraged Briggs to move his family across the continent so they could live nearby.

Briggs traveled to California to find out about job prospects. He stayed with Charles's family for four months while he studied possibilities and met business contacts. He liked what he saw and was welcomed by local businessmen.

By the time Beatrice's father returned to New England from California, he had decided to move his family to the West Coast. In spring 1891, he traveled back to California to stay. In June, Minnie and fifteen-year-old Beatrice moved across the country to join him.

The family took up residence in Paso Robles, an agricultural town known for fruit and almond orchards, and for a popular natural hot springs resort hotel. Beatrice's family adopted the *Farnum* spelling of their last name while they lived on the West Coast. Beatrice, who had always gone by her middle name, was often listed as "F. B. Farnum" or "F. Beatrice Farnum" in printed documents.

Beatrice enrolled in the newly established Paso Robles High School. In 1895, during her senior year, nineteen-year-old Beatrice worked as a clerk in the post office where her father was postmaster.

In 1896, Beatrice graduated after four years of high school as part of the first graduating class of Paso Robles High School. She and another young woman were the school's first female graduates. Her commencement speech, "An Air Castle," appeared on the front page of *The Paso Robles Leader* on July 1, 1896. She was twenty years old. The article, a tribute to the young woman's accomplishments, was read widely by residents of Paso Robles.

In her speech, Beatrice gave a journalistic account of her graduation trip to Hawaii. Her buoyant essay described the natural beauty she observed:

Surely this is some fairy land! It could never be the lot of mortals to inhabit such bright shores. . . . Without doubt the islands have the distinction of presenting to the view of man the most sublime of earthly spectacles and natural phenomena.

Beatrice and fellow graduate, Alberta Bell, pictured in
The Paso Robles Leader on July 1, 1896.
Courtesy of Paso Robles Historical Society.

In a sentimental aside, Beatrice noted, "Perhaps there is a momentary sadness as familiar faces fade from view but new surroundings soon claim the attention." She resumed describing her excitement as the ship cruised "through the Golden Gate onto the broad Pacific." Her writing revealed her developing adventurous spirit, a passion for travel, and her appreciation of natural beauty, views, and landscapes.

Soon after high school graduation, she and her mother traveled to San Francisco to enroll Beatrice in the Mark Hopkins Institute of Art, for instruction in fine arts, music, and literature. The Hopkins Mansion, which housed the school, was donated in 1893 to the University of California in trust for the San Francisco Art Institute. The Hopkins Mansion was a visible landmark atop Telegraph Hill in San Francisco.

Following Beatrice to San Francisco, her parents moved to

the bustling city during the midst of its burgeoning art culture. The close-knit family shared a flat in downtown San Francisco while supporting Beatrice through her art school studies.

The following summer, Beatrice and her mother returned to Paso Robles for the 1897 Fourth of July parade. They received attention in the July 7, 1896, *Paso Robles Leader* for the artistically decorated horse-drawn carriage they had created and driven in the parade. Beatrice and Minnie wore white satin attire and won a prize for locally grown clematis flower bunting on their carriage, as well as red, white, and blue decorations on their horse's harness.

For the next five years, while she studied art at the Hopkins Institute, Beatrice and her parents lived on Larkin Street in San Francisco. Their residence was near a streetcar line on a route to the art school located on Telegraph Hill. In San Francisco's city directories, Beatrice was listed as an art student, artist, and portrait artist. Her skill as a portrait artist would have added to the

A postcard shows the Mark Hopkins Institute of Art,
San Francisco, before 1906.

household income. Her father worked as a grocery salesman and clerk.

In August 1903, Charles Farnum, who had helped and encouraged her family to move to California, died from tuberculosis. Beatrice was twenty-seven years old when he passed away. She had finished art school and made plans to move back east with her family, where she could explore options for her design and artwork.

A notice in *The Paso Robles Leader* on July 20, 1904, stated, "Mr. and Mrs. B. C. Farnum have lately gone East where Beatrice has selected a beautiful home for them at South Weymouth, within 35 miles of Boston. These people will be remembered as former residents of this place."

By July 1904, Briggs, Minnie, and Beatrice had moved and again lived on the East Coast. They had reverted to the *Farnham* spelling of their surname, as favored by their eastern relatives. Living close to Boston and New York City gave Beatrice access to agents and galleries and opportunities to build a client base.

Two years later in 1906, San Francisco's Great Earthquake destroyed much of the city. The Hopkins Institute of Art and the adjacent Hopkins Mansion were destroyed, with only a charred cluster of vertical pillars remaining. Records and artwork at the Institute were destroyed by the fire ignited by the devastating earthquake. No record of Beatrice's years at the Institute and none of her artwork survived the fire.

Although several newspaper articles reported that Beatrice lived in New York City for five years following her return to the East, her family's Massachusetts address was listed as her official residence in the 1907 South Weymouth City Directory and the 1910 U.S. Census. She likely took the train to New York City to meet with art dealers, gallery owners, and interior design clients.

During the February 26, 1911, *St. Louis Post-Dispatch* interview, Beatrice expressed opinions about women in business and her views on her travels:

> The trouble with most women who go into business, they are too narrow of vision. . . . economizing on necessities and physical comforts, the fundamentals of success. I used to see them in the studios in New York, skimping along doing without their breakfast or luncheons, struggling always, looking neither to the right or the left of them, never taking a vacation.
>
> Now, the very moment my last big order for the holiday trade is finished, without a thought of preparation, I take the first train out of South Weymouth and hit the sunset trail.

As her passion for western art and culture continued to grow, Beatrice relished train travel to New Mexico and Arizona. On her cross-country trip in 1910, she discovered new sights, purchased Native American arts and crafts, and studied Indigenous culture. She balanced her need to be in the East for business reasons and the cultural immersion that inspired her in the West. Sharing a household with her parents made maintaining that balance financially feasible.

On January 27, 1911, *The Albuquerque Morning Journal* reported on Beatrice's outdoor garb, which included a cowboy hat, coat, gloves, and a large leather bag decorated with beads. The writer remarked, "It's rather strange attire for a New York artist whose household decorations grace the homes of millionaires—whose earnings have enabled her to buy a summer home in South Weymouth, Mass., which was pictured in a leading periodical of the country but—it suits Beatrice Farnham."

Because of her tanned complexion and western attire, Beatrice was described as being of Native American descent. She responded with unhidden sarcasm:

A woman writer in a New York paper had a 'story' one day about my trip each year to the tribe of my people where I got the queer mystic designs which I use in my work. Since I am [supposedly] accepted as a member of a tribe I am trying to find out the name of a good bunch of Indians—perhaps you can suggest one?

Beatrice also deplored the parsing of the wild and woolly westerner in eastern literature:

These types exist only in books in the minds of those who have never been out west. . . . They are disappointed when they come west and find the people merely civilized and human as anywhere. In literature the western story still holds first place. I find my success with Indian designs and find the queer symbols of the Indians are what the people want in the bungalow homes which are the American rage at present.

A month later, in *The St. Louis Post-Dispatch* of February 26, 1911, she elaborated on her travels:

People tell me I'm extravagant, taking three months vacation in the winter season and going out there to loaf on horseback with a lot of Indians, when I might be studying in cultivated Europe or New York and reading up Indian lore in libraries. None of that must and dust for me.

I attribute the fact that I have been more successful and in shorter time than most women who go into business to just such knowledge as I acquire sitting out there blinking in the sun.

During the years she lived in South Weymouth, Beatrice often visited friends and relatives around the country. She bought a motorboat to give her adventurous spirit an outlet, and she piloted it alone to Cincinnati on the Ohio River.

When Beatrice brought her restless spirit to the river waterways, she attracted attention in *Collier's: The National Weekly* on May 28, 1910. An article in a section entitled "Women To-Day—News of Her Activities—Domestic, Political, and Intellectual" described her adventures:

Miss Beatrice Farnham
Who navigates the inland
waters in her own motor boat

A Massachusetts girl, Beatrice Farnham by name, and an artist as well as a girl, is investigating our great river highways by means of her own motor-boat. She runs the *Aloha* herself, has covered hundreds of miles on the Ohio and its tributaries, and contemplates going down the Mississippi on her next outing. Her mascot is a chantecler, who swam the Illinois River on the latest tour and was rescued by a life-saving crew.

Collier's Weekly, May 28, 1910

CHAPTER 3

John Otto, Trail Builder

Beatrice's pal John Otto, who had given her the gold bracelet, built trails in western Colorado, but was born and raised in the Midwest. His Prussian-born parents, Karl "Emil" Otto and Amalie (or Amelia) Otto, had migrated from Saxony, Germany to Wisconsin. The family later settled in Marthasville, Missouri, a community called Charrette by early explorers and settlers. The 1880 U.S. Census lists their children as Hermen, twelve, John, nine, Clara, seven, Taleta, five, and Emil, two.

Emil Otto taught theology at Evangelical Missouri College, later renamed Eden Theological Seminary. He was well-known for his progressive ideas and theological interpretations. When he was censured by church leaders who did not agree with his ideas, he resigned from his position in Missouri. By 1890, he had accepted a teaching job at Elmhurst College, west of Chicago.

John briefly studied religion and music at Elmhurst College. Considered a free thinker and a vocal political individualist, he did not settle in for long at Elmhurst. Within a year, John left college and his home in the Midwest.

In the 1890s, he traveled west to prospect for gold in California. He wandered up the Pacific coast to northern California, where he found mining work in Siskiyou County. By 1900, he resided in Oak Bar, California where his age was incorrectly recorded in the census as twenty-six instead of twenty-nine. As a miner, he learned to excavate rugged rocky terrain and how to use dynamite and other explosives. He earned respect as a dependable worker and would use his mining skills the rest of his life.

In 1902, John was detained by California police when he did not pay a merchant for a pair of work trousers. He had confused a clerk with rambling rhetoric about a campaign to promote volunteerism before he left the shop without paying. When his erratic behavior continued, he was detained by the sheriff and sent for a few weeks to Napa State Hospital, where his mental health was evaluated.

When he was released, John left California behind. He drifted to Idaho to attempt prospecting. He then moved on to try his luck in mining districts in Colorado. While working odd jobs and panning for gold, he witnessed unrest among miners and labor strikes due to mismanagement, inhumane conditions, long work hours, and unsafe mines. He sympathized with the miners.

In 1903 during a time of mining strikes and labor upheaval, John rented a room in Denver, Colorado's capital city. While there, he wrote repeated notes to Governor James H. Peabody, demanding a meeting with him. John advocated for an eight-hour workday and presented other ideas to improve working conditions for all miners.

John was adamant about expressing his opinions vocally and in writing. His numerous notes, letters and repeated rambling rhetoric to the Colorado governor became an unrelenting nuisance until John was considered an unstable public threat.

When John was finally granted an appointment to meet with

JOHN OTTO,
Socialist Who Gave Governor Bad Scare.

Rocky Mountain News, **November 16, 1903**

the governor at the capitol building in November 1903, detectives detained him. A miner's candlestick on a sharpened steel spike, retrieved from his pocket, was perceived as a dangerous weapon. John's erratic behavior added to the detectives' concerns about him, and he was arrested. After a couple of weeks in jail, he was released as a harmless crank.

Upon his release, he wrote a statement that was published in *The Rocky Mountain News* on November 19, 1903:

Dear Sir.—"P stands for prisoner. L stands for liberty. I have been released from prison this morning. P stands for peaceful—as a peaceful citizen I will continue to uphold the law. P stands for Pinkertons [a private police force that targeted striking miners]. I will politely inform them that I will not cross Broadway. Please take this as a 'peace proclamation.' Yours, truly,   JOHN OTTO.

For the next few years, John drifted among Colorado mining camps. In 1906 he arrived in the Grand Valley of western Colorado to work on a construction crew. The workers were hired to build a twenty-two-mile-long wooden flume to transport water from a high mesa reservoir to the town of Fruita.

John had found a place to settle.

Ute tribes lived and hunted in the Grand Valley long before eastern settlers arrived in the late 1800s. The Ute people camped in the valley and hunted in the high mountain terrain on the Uncompahgre Plateau and the nearby Grand Mesa, a vast flat-topped mountain. Utes migrated through the mountains and canyons. Game killed in the high country provided much of their food.

When eastern pioneers crossed the Rocky Mountains to settle in the Grand Valley, skirmishes and conflicts with Ute tribes erupted. In spite of efforts to maintain peace from both sides, government treaties were broken. Warriors protecting their homelands retaliated for the encroachment of settlers. By 1880, all local Ute tribes had been forced to leave the Grand Valley and relocate to the Uintah and Ouray Reservation, in the Uintah Basin of Utah.

The town of Grand Junction was founded in the Grand

Valley in 1881. As the hub of five railroad routes, the town grew and prospered. Grand Junction also benefited from its location at the confluence of the Gunnison River and the Grand River (renamed the Colorado River in 1923). The Grand River, which flows west of Grand Junction to the town of Fruita, twelve miles away, continues on to Utah.

In 1906, when John arrived to work in the Grand Valley, he was amazed to discover hidden canyons, stunning cliffs, and rock formations rimmed by high mesas near the construction site. The awe-inspiring landscape covered more than thirty square miles of wilderness. A few miles away from the rugged canyons, the Grand River (later renamed the Colorado River) flowed through the valley.

Exploring the canyons was not easy, except on trails created by Ute migration and wildlife paths near the river. Steep, rocky inclines led to high mesas to the south. A labyrinth of dark canyons and gulches lay beneath high rim rocks. Wildlife trails

**Main Street, Grand Junction, Colorado, prior to automobile traffic.
Postcard circa 1910.**

meandered toward the mesa from the river, gaining elevation through rocks, juniper bushes, low-growing prickly pear cactius, and spiky yucca plants.

Residents in the twenty-five-year-old community of Grand Junction were hardly aware of the nearby secluded canyons, rock formations, and amazing views. For them to visit the area, trails with steep elevation gain would need to be cleared and developed for passage on horseback, in horse-drawn wagons, or on foot.

Enchanted by the area, John was determined to build trails to make the remote area accessible to nearby residents. He spent his free time building new trails, never requesting payment for his labor. As he worked, he began to dream about preserving the area as a national park. He began a letter-writing campaign focused on the development of a national park to protect the area and allow access to all people.

When construction work was completed for Fruita's water supply, John decided to stay. He is quoted in the *Colorado National Monument Map and Guide* in a section titled *One Man's Dream*.

"I came here last year and found these canyons, and they felt like the heart of the world to me," John wrote in 1907. "I'm going to stay . . . and promote this place because it should be a national park." John had found his place and his purpose. He set up camp and made the canyons his home.

In 1906, Mesa Verde, with vestiges of the homes of ancient Indigenous tribes, was the latest of seven national parks by then established in the United States, and the only national park in Colorado. National parks, created by an act of Congress for the purpose of providing inspiration, education, and recreation, had to be large enough for effective administration and wide-scale use.

John Otto leads a pack burro on a high canyon trail.
Courtesy of Colorado National Monument, U.S. Park Service.

The Antiquities Act in 1906 allowed U.S. presidents to "declare by public proclamation historic landmarks, historic and prehistoric structures, and other objects of historic or scientific interest that are situated upon the lands owned or controlled by the Government of the United States to be national monuments." A national monument was not the same as a national park, the creation of which would have required an act of Congress.

John was convinced that his secluded canyons, the area he called Monument Park, was deserving of national park designation and preservation for all citizens.

John cleared and created paths, making the canyons easier for visitors to reach on foot or by riding surefooted trail horses. He enlarged trails—created by deer and other animals seeking foliage, berries, and precious water close to the river—to make them accessible on horseback.

When John worked in the springtime, temperatures were mild in the high desert. Occasional rain brought welcome water to nearby gulches, most of which received only six to eight inches of precipitation annually. As spring continued, water became sparse, and small canyon streams turned into dry gulches. As summer progressed, temperatures nudged well into the 90s.

For three years, from 1906 to 1909, John lived in a secluded area that became known as Monument Canyon. He moved camp according to weather, the water supply, food caches, feed for his trail animals, access to caves, and his work on trails and other projects. Monument Canyon stretched about three miles with over 1,000-foot elevation gain along paths following the Colorado River from Grand Junction to Fruita.

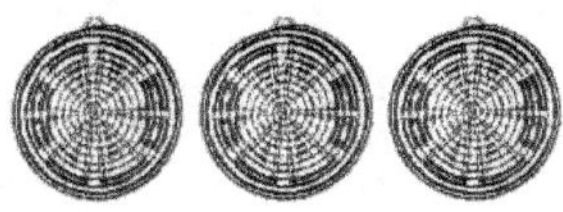

Enchanted by the terrain, John named some stone structures for presidents, such as Lincoln, Jefferson, and Washington. Many of his names did not last, and others were added. Balanced Rock, Coke Ovens, and Independence Monument became popular enduring landmarks.

Independence Rock, later called Independence Monument, was a freestanding five-hundred-foot-tall solitary rock formation of rusty red-yellow sandstone with a flat cap rock at the top. Surrounded by shadowed canyons, Independence Monument changed with different lighting, creating various moods as the sun's rays shifted throughout the day.

When John set up camp near Independence Monument, he was intrigued by the looming size and shape of the formation. He wanted to climb to the top, install a sturdy flagpole among rocks at the precipice, and fly the largest American flag he could obtain. He also hoped someday to shoot off four sticks of dynamite from the top to celebrate the Fourth of July.

Such formidable tasks might have been daunting to anybody other than John Otto, but he was determined to accomplish the climb and build a ladder to the top of the monolith. Independence Monument was the centerpiece of his work. It also increased his resolve to establish and preserve the area as a national park.

John pursued his campaign to draw attention to the canyons. He expounded his opinions in letters to newspapers, encouraging all citizens to visit and benefit from the scenic beauty and the majesty of nature available to them. His days were filled with work on the trails so that others could access and enjoy the canyons.

The newspaper office at *The Grand Junction Daily Sentinel* was a regular stop for John when he came to town. His friends on the news staff printed most of his long-winded descriptions of life on the trail and his strident opinions on many subjects. John's

Independence Monument

friends and supporters among newspaper readers were interested and amused. Others tired of reading his essays, especially when they became rambling and confusing.

John did not often go to Grand Junction and was sometimes absent from town for weeks at a time. His secluded campground in Monument Canyon was around twelve miles west of the city. Friends who lived in town appreciated visiting John at his camp. Some visitors brought a picnic meal and spent the day outdoors exploring, hiking, climbing, and sometimes helping John with projects.

Neighbors in the community of Glade Park, located on a high mesa adjacent to the canyons, collected John's mail for him. When John stopped by to visit, he caught up on news and correspondence. He was known to many as a courteous, amiable, educated, and interesting person, who took friends on tours and offered help when assistance was needed. Memories of his past

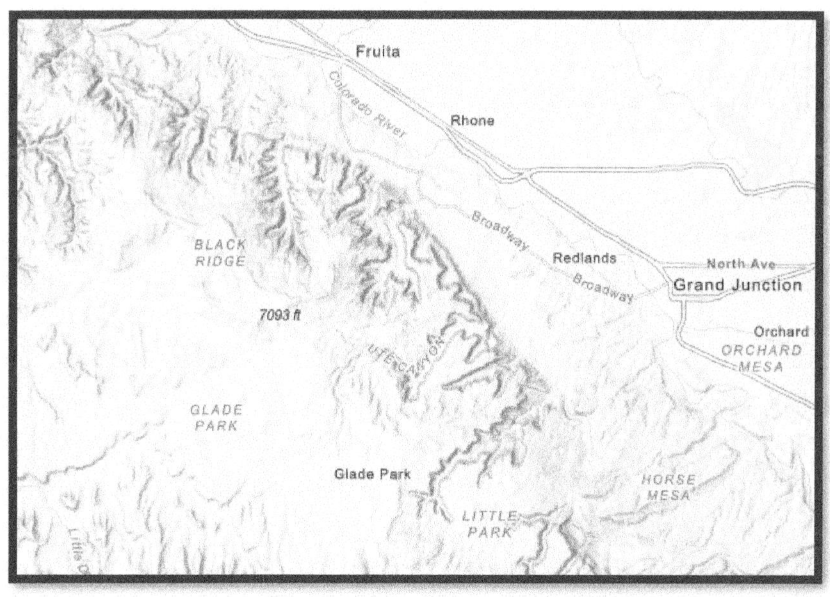

Topographical map showing Grand Junction, Fruita, Glade Park, and the canyons and other terrain of Colorado National Monument. *Courtesy of ArcGIS.*

troubles with the law faded as he continued to work on trails, and to lobby for Monument National Park. John's admirers perceived him as an intelligent, eccentric engineer of outdoor resources, who enjoyed displaying the American flag and setting off fireworks with patriotic zeal.

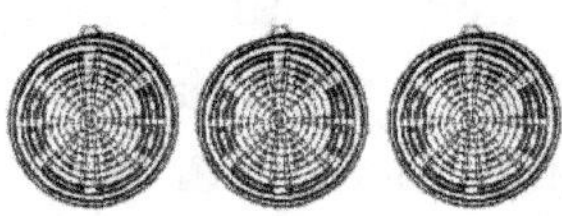

John worked tirelessly without pay, performing odd jobs for food and money. Friends and backers grubstaked him with funds for supplies so he could continue his work. He took on a few side jobs, including constructing trails on nearby Grand Mesa, and he accepted tips for leading visitors on canyon tours and guiding hunting parties. He also worked picking fruit in the fall.

Despite his work in the canyons, John continued to fight for changes in Colorado's mining laws. In 1907, John expressed his dissatisfaction with mining labor laws to Colorado's new governor, Henry A. Buchtel. John was arrested and sent to jail when he threatened to set off dynamite in the town of Fruita if the governor appeared there to speak at the Fourth of July celebration.

When John appeared in court in Grand Junction in February 1908, friends testified on his behalf. The jury declared him not guilty, and Judge Sullivan, who oversaw the case, released John from jail. Although John was declared sane at the hearing, he was considered unstable by many.

The Grand Junction Daily Sentinel in Grand Junction reported on February 24, 1908, "Otto appeared calm and quiet to the court room today . . . While he is perfectly sane on many subjects, on other subjects he is decidedly mentally unbalanced."

During the trial, newspapers dubbed him the "Monument Canon Hermit," and he developed a statewide reputation. After the trial, he retreated to the solitude of his campsite in the shadows of the area that would eventually become Colorado National Monument. He resumed his work, building trails without payment, and lived in a tent, teepee, or cave, with his horse, burros, and dogs nearby.

Although he was known as a recluse or hermit, John was considered amiable and personable in his interactions with friends, neighbors, and anybody who expressed interest in hearing about his work in the canyons. He was always willing to guide people to the natural wonders that existed a few miles from town.

A June 28, 1908, letter to the *Daily Sentinel* told of John's plan to guide Chamber of Commerce members from Fruita and Grand Junction through "National Monument Park," to gain official support for the yet unnamed park. He had a new idea for a "National Cooperation Day—on the last Sunday in June and each year thereafter to forever promote its principles, etc. etc."

John Otto photo in *Collier's: The National Weekly, July 1, 1911.*

This new plan was apparently meant to encourage an alliance of local city officials and residents for stronger support of the national park project. The *Daily Sentinel* described the message as a "characteristic and interesting letter from John Otto, 'the hermit of Monument canon,' a man whose eccentricities have puzzled many people."

John was a good choice for a trail guide. He enjoyed talking to visitors, sharing his knowledge of the area, and boosting his vision to establish a national park. He was often rewarded with tips, which he needed for supplies and food. In 1910, John guided his artist friend Beatrice Farnham, to the best scenic views for painting landscapes.

For five years, John's work was difficult and lonely at times. He appreciated friends who came to see him, especially when they helped him with chores. However, he was hoping to find a partner to share his toil and his victories. He wanted somebody who would commit to stay with him long-term. Sooner would be better than later.

Hikers in Monument Canyon with a guide.
Postcard circa 1910.

CHAPTER 4

A National Monument

John's campaign to promote the wild, rugged terrain and rock formations did not go unnoticed. He sent numerous letters to *The Grand Junction Daily Sentinel* and to politicians, including William H. Taft, U.S. president from 1909 to 1913, following Theodore Roosevelt's term.

John's efforts to promote a national park gained momentum in 1909. The Grand Junction Chamber of Commerce met that year with an agent from the Midland Railroad, which connected Colorado Springs to Grand Junction. The railroad sent an official photographer to take pictures of Monument Park. Denver and Rio Grande (D&RG) Railroad officials were also invited to send a photographer. Publicity photos would provide Grand Junction and railroad companies with scenic images to attract tourists. John was available and eager to guide photographers to the best vistas in the canyons.

When John discovered cold underground springs in Monument Park, the Grand Junction Chamber of Commerce had the water tested to determine if it was safe for drinking. The water was safe, and the springs were named Evergreen Spring and

Good Luck Spring. Now visitors and pack animals in the park had a reliable source of water. Townspeople who drank from the springs were impressed by the quality of the water. A sample of water from the springs was even delivered to *The Daily Sentinel*.

John wrote a letter on May 17, 1909, to President Taft, inviting him to visit Grand Junction to view the beautiful sights of Monument Park during his upcoming cross-country train tour. His letter was reprinted on May 27, 1909, in *The Daily Sentinel*.

My Dear President:

If it is in any way possible on your proposed trip this summer to stop over at Grand Junction in the Grand valley, Colorado, by all thats [*sic*] true, please do so, and inspect the National Monument Park, which then we hope through a decree (an order to have it set aside) from you shall be known as the Monument National Park.

Yours respectfully,

John Otto.

When a week later he received a reply on White House stationery, John wasted no time riding his horse into Grand Junction. He shared the letter and his excitement with the newspaper staff.

The message from President Taft became local news on May 27, 1909, when the *Daily Sentinel* printed both John's letter and the president's response. The headline read, "Otto Receives Letter from Pres. Taft." The correspondence, which acknowledged John Otto's invitation, was signed by the president's secretary. The letter stated that Taft had "not yet determined whether it will be possible to make a Western trip, but should he conclude to go, he will be glad to give careful consideration to your wishes."

On September 22, 1909, Taft visited the Grand Valley on his

western tour. He was the honored guest at the Mesa County Fair where he met the Peach Queen, a young lady with attendants chosen to reign at the fall harvest celebration. A carton of peaches was presented to the president. John and Monument Park were not included on the president's itinerary, but Taft sent an American flag to Otto, which was set aside to use later in Monument Park.

On December 9, 1909, in a narrow column above *The Daily Sentinels* banner, was a short news item titled, "Saved to the People." Colorado's congressional delegation had recommended "Monument canon and park" to be considered for a national park. The column applauded John's intrepid unselfishness:

> To no other person is the credit due for having saved that great piece of national domain which vies with the most beautiful natural parks in the country for scenic beauty. . . . John Otto has accomplished this work single-handed and alone. He has dug trails, opened up roads and toiled with his hands, heart and mind to accomplish this for the people. The day of gratitude will grow for John Otto from the people of this city.

With a headline reading, "Deserve Aid from County," *The Daily Sentinel* on December 21, 1909, boosted John's accomplishments by suggesting that county commissioners appropriate $100 to John for his "great and noble work" of trail building and to help pay for needed supplies.

The newspaper also suggested that individuals pay a subscription fee to Otto based on the financial and community gain that Monument Park would provide local citizens in the future. The article said, "John Otto is in town today for the first time in several weeks and in spite of the cold weather he has worked almost daily on the trail. . . . He had worked unaided to build a remarkable [trail] five or six miles in length overcoming untold obstacles and without having the assistance of laborers."

The newspaper reported on December 21, 1909, "Citizens appreciative of Otto's work have made $1.00 subscriptions from time to time to Otto to aid him in buying tools, powder, provisions, etc., but the total sum of these contributions have not exceeded $10." Whether additional subscriptions were collected or not, John must have been uplifted by the show of support from the newspaper staff.

But support for John was slow in coming. John continued to guide tours and traded labor for supplies. When Beatrice Farnham visited the Grand Valley in 1910, John was hired as her guide. He led her to views of steep cliffs and solid rock formations with shifting shadows and light at every turn in the high desert terrain.

Monument Canyon

In correspondence with Beatrice after her 1910 visit, John encouraged her to return to the valley the following spring. Apparently the two developed a partnership during her visit. Perhaps John hinted in his letters that he hoped the eastern artist would arrive and stay. If the relationship developed, he would no longer live alone as "The Hermit in the Canyon."

John continued to send in progress reports to newspapers regarding the five to six miles of trails he constructed through rocky canyons. To help with John's dream of a national park, approximately 350 local citizens signed a petition. This document was sent to President Taft, encouraging him to designate the area known as Monument Park as a national park.

On May 24, 1911, John's work finally paid off. President Taft signed proclamation no. 1126, establishing "Colorado National Monument" on 20,500 acres of canyon wilderness.

The previously used name of Monolithic National Monument did not sit well. Nor was it clear to many if the area was a national park or a national monument. While officials tried to determine a rightful name and category, the designation changed frequently. City officials in Grand Junction ruminated over a final name, which required their approval.

In response to a call for names for the park, one fanciful suggestion was "Smith". The idea was attributed to John Otto, who had grown impatient with the naming process. He reasoned that everybody with the common surname Smith would be eager to visit the Grand Valley and the new park.

After a process of trial and error, the park was eventually named Colorado National Monument. As a result of his efforts, John was offered the position as the monument's first custodian. He accepted the job. The position paid a salary of one dollar per month.

A few miles away from the new national monument, the Grand River continued its flow west with mountain snow melt.

The wooden flume that John and others had built a few years earlier transported precious water from high mesa reservoirs to the town of Fruita. Irrigation ditches allowed farmers to grow crops in increasingly bountiful apple and peach orchards.

The Grand Valley was growing. Harvested produce was transported by inter-urban railroads from orchards to Grand Junction and then shipped to distant locations. John anticipated that the railroad, which brought his eastern artist trail friend to the Grand Valley in 1910, would bring her back again the following spring.

CHAPTER 5

The Grand Valley

After she sat for days on a westbound train from Boston to Colorado, Beatrice was more than ready to stretch her legs and stand on solid ground. She received a respite in Pueblo, Colorado, at the foot of the Rocky Mountains. There westbound passengers from the Atchison, Topeka, and Santa Fe Railroad had to change to the Denver and Rio Grande's "baby railroad." Weary travelers could walk around the station for a break from the rumbling ride. The brick platform felt solid to legs that were shaky from train travel.

Beatrice had plenty of time to contemplate her excursion during her travels. The February trip to New Mexico, when she had celebrated her thirty-fifth birthday, seemed like long ago. During her previous trip, she'd ridden across desert plains on horseback, and talked with Native American crafters about their art. She felt a kinship to the indigenous people who kindly shared their designs and symbols, which she duplicated for decorations. She'd returned home with new ideas and to visit with family, art agents, and clients. However, she was soon restless to return to the West.

During the winter of 1911, Beatrice must have pondered her return trip to western Colorado in the spring. The previous summer, John Otto had escorted her on horseback to the best views for painting landscapes. A comfortable friendship had developed. In February, when she'd been interviewed by Marguerite Martyn in St. Louis, Beatrice had fondly described John as "a forest ranger" and "a mighty fine pal." Perhaps he was interested in using her artwork to promote his campaign for a national park in the canyons. If they shared trails and mutual goals, an enduring partnership might develop beyond the designation of "a mighty fine pal". The prospect was intriguing. She was soon aboard another westbound train. This time, her destination was the Grand Valley in western Colorado.

At that time, the D&RG line through the mountains used

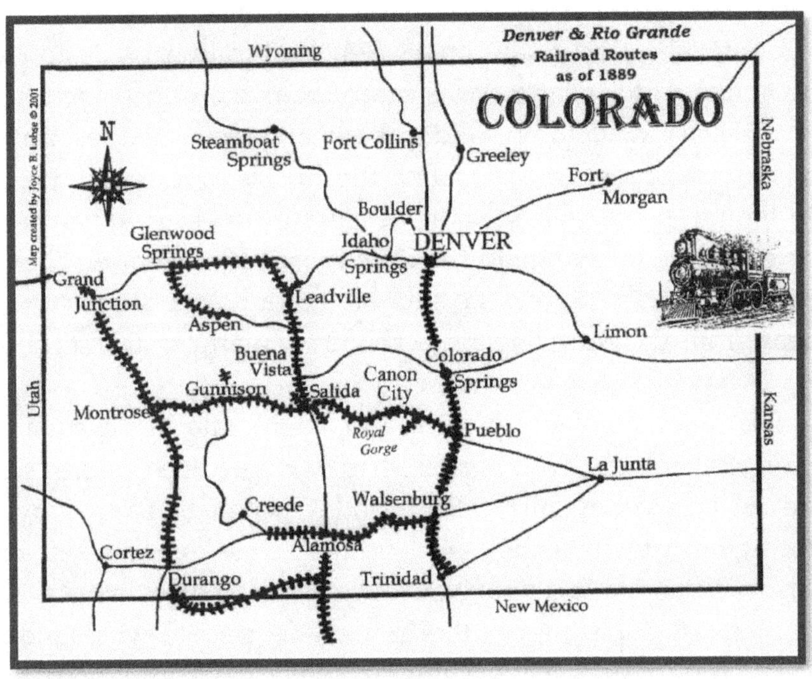

The Denver & Rio Grande Railroad routes in Colorado in 1880.
Reprinted from General William Palmer: Railroad Pioneer,
Filter Press, 2009.

narrow gauge tracks, constructed three feet apart rather than standard configuration of four feet, eight and a half inches. Smaller trains on narrow tracks were better able to navigate steep climbs and tight curves through rugged terrain and elevations.

Standard gauge routes, which navigated around mountain peaks and valleys instead of through them, required more time for travel. Narrow gauge railroads curved and climbed steep, winding grades high across the rugged Rocky Mountains, covering fewer miles. Passengers were encouraged to enjoy the scenic views and stunning vistas.

The D&RG line westbound from Pueblo followed the Arkansas River between tall rocky cliffs and through the twelve-hundred-foot-deep Royal Gorge. West of Salida, the narrow gauge route split. The northbound track headed over higher elevation, and crossed the Continental Divide to the Leadville mining district. The westbound route traversed pine-forested mountain ranges and foothills across high desert plains. At Montrose, the route turned north toward Grand Junction, where the Gunnison River connected to the Grand River.

Although John was known as an eccentric recluse who lived in caves and canyons, Beatrice was motivated to return to the Grand Valley to visit her trail guide again. In spite of his past difficulties with the law, she admired his resolve, hard work, and intelligence. His efforts to build trails and create a national park were unselfish and unrelenting. Perhaps further study of the unusual canyons and rock formations with the quirky trail builder would fulfill her search for a place to settle in the West.

Beatrice was intrigued by the terrain's similarities to parts of New Mexico. High desert plants and cacti in sandy soil were surrounded by rugged sagebrush, jagged rock formations, and low, crooked trees with tough roots, forever searching for water.

Her ideas were also evolving regarding her desire to help

young women learn to be independent, as she had become, and to learn healthy outdoor living skills. The western canyons might provide a fine location for a young woman's retreat. Possibilities were intriguing and provided food for thought as hours on the train slipped away with the miles.

As an artist, Beatrice embraced Colorado's vast open spaces, visible from train windows during her journey. Although the changing scenery was remarkable, she must have been eager to reach her destination in western Colorado's Grand Valley to see how her plans would unfold.

When the train arrived at Grand Junction's Union Depot, steel wheels screeched and steam hissed to slow the engine's approach. After the train jerked to a stop, the porter jumped to the platform to set up a wooden step to help tired passengers alight from the rail cars. Beatrice, careful not to trip on the hem of her long skirt, was assisted to the ground by the porter.

Grand Junction was home to about eight thousand residents in 1911. The town was located about thirty miles east of the Utah border and was situated at an altitude of 4,593 feet. The area's economy was sustained by mining, ranching, and irrigation farming. Crops of apples, pears, peaches, grapes, and sugar beets were abundant.

An impressive two-story Italian Renaissance train station, completed five years earlier, accommodated growing railroad traffic in Grand Junction. Initial construction costs were about $60,000 (equal to about $2,040,000 a century later). The station boasted white brick stonework, a red tile roof, terra cotta ornamentation, marble counters, stained glass panels in high windows, and solid golden oak benches, doors, and trim. The Grand Junction Union Depot was considered one of the finest railroad stations in the West.

The train terminal had opened on April 17, 1906, the date of

Grand Junction Union Depot, postcard circa 1910.

the disastrous San Francisco earthquake. Many California residents rode the rails east to escape the devastation and rested at the new Grand Junction Union Depot. Residents set up a relief site and provided food, clothing, bedding, and medical care. After its illustrious beginning as a sanctuary for earthquake victims, the new train station thrived.

Beatrice was accustomed to elegant train stations and hotels. If John was not present when she arrived, she planned to stay at the La Court Hotel, which provided a horse-drawn buggy to pick up arrivals at the station. Travelers and cargo then took a short ride from the depot to Second and Main Streets.

The La Court provided food, lodging, a hot bath, and a place to write letters and telegrams. It was near diners, livery stables, and street cars. Later that summer, Beatrice would befriend the owners of the La Court and offer her design services for the hotel's upcoming renovation.

As Beatrice disembarked from the train, she must have looked forward to her return to the canyons west of Grand

Junction to paint scenery and explore new vistas. She was also eager to learn more about John's plans in the rugged territory he proudly referred to as "The Heart of the World." She might also have wondered if her travels, maybe even her future hopes, were part of a fool's errand.

Her plans were evolving. She hoped to create new artwork to sell back in Boston. She planned to teach young women the skills necessary to become independent. She also intended to settle down and make the West her home. But would John be part of her future?

Beatrice liked rugged, straightforward, western men. John was an intelligent, independent, and strong outdoorsman of the type she favored. Perhaps they both could combine their skills and aspirations by working together in the wild, inspiring place he called Monument Park, surrounded by rocky cliffs and canyon shadows.

PART 2

You get a breadth of view in the big open spaces, and it is mental as well as physical. You get a perspective of yourself. You see just how small you are—and maybe it's the bracing air, for health is the greatest inspiration after all. But something fires you with ambition to come back and beat the world.
Beatrice Farnham
St. Louis Post-Dispatch, February 26, 1911

CHAPTER 6

Independence Monument

When Beatrice arrived in Grand Junction in spring 1911, activity was buzzing. John was on the brink of achieving his goal to establish Monument Park as a national preserve.

John's base camp was about thirteen miles from town, in a large canyon on the west side of the park. Beatrice knew that John might not be there when her train arrived. If he wasn't, she could use her time alone to send messages, pick up supplies, eat a warm meal, take a bath, and get a good night of rest before she left town. A nearby livery stable rented horses, with or without a buggy or wagon. At that time, residents could still stand and talk in the middle of Main Street without worries about automobile traffic.

When she arrived, she must have been pleased to see her pal and trail guide waiting to greet her and take her to his camp. At John's camp, two separate tents were positioned a respectable

Independence Monument, circa 1940. Dean photo, Agfa/Ansco postcard.

forty feet apart, in a vague attempt at propriety. Nearby, the sheer stone edifice Independence Monument loomed over them like a chaperone.

Once settled in, Beatrice easily slipped into her own routine at the campsite. She helped with chores, tended to the pack animals, and put out food and water for the dogs. John, who was accustomed to living alone, welcomed her willingness to help and to cook some meals. Beatrice, always the artist, studied surrounding cliffs and rock formations for potential subjects to use in artwork.

The name Independence was one of many patriotic labels John had attached to landmarks. For a long time, he had been determined to ascend the top of the towering Independence Monument, which reached skyward more than five hundred feet from its foundation on the canyon floor. Now that Beatrice had joined him in his camp, he hoped he would finally succeed.

Looking up at Independence Monument from the base, where Beatrice might have stood

Independence Monument loomed as a sentinel, a guardian, a warden, and an intruder over their camp. Its moods changed from bright to dark, throwing shadows across the canyon. The reddish-brown rock varied in color throughout the day as the sky changed from brightness to cloudiness to darkness. When brightness faded, the monolith adapted a cloak of gloomy gray during turbulent weather or approaching nighttime, especially when clouds blocked the sun, moon and stars.

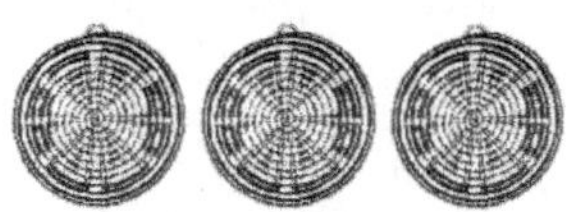

Shortly after her arrival in the Grand Valley, Beatrice accepted John's proposal of marriage. John was forty years old, and Beatrice was thirty-five. They had corresponded since her visit the previous summer and saw no reason to hesitate.

John presented Beatrice with a pack burro named Foxy as a wedding gift. As a sensible northeastern woman, she was pleased by the practicality of the gift, which was more useful to her than a ring. Foxy was to be a welcome companion, to carry her tools and art supplies on trails through the canyons.

In keeping with his practice of writing and distributing public statements, John shared his excitement about his engagement to Miss Beatrice Farnham by sending cards and letters to newspaper offices. Telegraph messages and United Press wire service spread the news quickly across the country. The May 5, 1911, *Mesa County Mail* wrote in an article titled "John Otto to Be Wed":

John Otto, trail builder, has fired a rocket into the air that will send its light all over the nation. It reads in letters of fire. "I am engaged to marry Miss Beatrice Farnham, an artist, who loves the wilds as I do and is content in the lovely hills and trails even as I."

. . . The remarkable woman of queenly stature and artistic temperament, who has won the heart of the bronzed trail builder of stoical patience is a native of far eastern Massachusetts.

The following day, on May 6, 1911, *The Palisade Tribune* stated that John was "about to take unto himself a bride . . . who will join Mr. Otto in his work at Monument canon." Wedding plans were underway, and the ceremony would take place outdoors in June, among the canyons of Monument Park.

John wrote a letter to *The Daily Sentinel* that was reprinted on

May Day, 1911. In his letter, John expressed his excitement about his engagement: "The other day 'my partner' arrived. Miss Beatrice Farnham, artist, trail girl of the Southwest. . . . To make a long story short, we announce our engagement, to be married after the flag raising on the Independence Tower in June." He added with a bit of humor that their engagement was, "the story of the guide, who couldn't be hired." This time Beatrice apparently did not pay for his guide services.

Beatrice's roots and upbringing on the East and West Coasts, as well as her recent repeated stays in the Southwest, were not mentioned in the article, but if praised her as an "artist, plainswoman, writer, and fresh air enthusiast," with a "nationwide reputation as a young woman of culture, ability, and taste." John described her as "a woman who is of the west and whom he has kept close to the heart throbs of the Rockies."

Beatrice was accustomed to public attention from newspapers, which followed her travels and adventures in the Southwest. However, when John publicized their wedding plans, the story was quickly picked up by publications nationwide. Conjecture and rumors about their upcoming outdoor nuptials were abundant. So Beatrice needed to act quickly to share the news of her engagement with her East Coast family.

When reporters asked John and Beatrice how they met, their answers were vague. They gave varied versions, sometimes saying they met in the East, other times on the West Coast, in the Southwest, or in the desert of New Mexico.

On New Years' Day in 1902, John was listed in *The San Francisco Call* as a guest at the Western Hotel. Whether planned or by coincidence, the lodging was located only a few blocks from the flat where Beatrice had lived with her parents during her years as a student at the Hopkins Art Institute. It is possible that they met at that time.

John also suggested they had met in northern California, at

Mount Shasta near Yreka, where he had once worked as a miner. Beatrice mentioned her time in Albuquerque and Las Vegas, New Mexico, and her rides across the desert, where she visited Native tribes.

Although they were not specific, the couple alluded to being well known to one another prior to her visits to western Colorado. Their vague responses about their first meeting might have been intended to protect privacy and reputation.

Once she settled into John's camp, Beatrice was interested in exploring views and painting landscapes. On May 2, 1911, *The Rocky Mountain News* reported that she was "in Monument park getting material for a series of paintings which she will exhibit in the East." John was focused on the establishment of the new national monument. He was also engrossed in building steps in stone to reach the top of Independence Monument, where he would install a flagpole, raise an American flag, and celebrate the new National Monument.

John recruited Beatrice for a special project using her skills as an artist. In the May Day article in *The Daily Sentinel* he boasted, "Miss Farnham will artistically inscribe on a big rock nearby, facing the rising sun, the facsimile of the original signatures of the signers of the Declaration of Independence." She agreed to apply the sculpting skills she had learned in art school to chisel wording from the last line of the Declaration of Independence with the names of signers in time for Independence Day.

The inscription carved into stone, an expression of John's patriotism, was no small chore. Accessing the flat top of the rock slab would require Beatrice to crawl and carry tools across the slanted, gritty surface. The rock was shaped and tilted like a sandstone roof. After the text was chiseled in all capital letters, they planned to fill the letters with concrete. This would provide contrast, legibility, and protection from exposure to the elements.

The text began along the highest edge of the rock, more than ten feet above the ground. The last sentence of the Declaration of Independence reads as follows: "AND FOR THE SUPPORT OF THIS DECLARATION, WITH A FIRM RELIANCE ON THE PROTECTION OF DIVINE PROVIDENCE, WE MUTUALLY PLEDGE TO EACH OTHER OUR LIVES, OUR FORTUNES AND OUR SACRED HONOR." Signatures of those who signed the document were chiseled below.

Unshielded from sunlight, wind, rain, and snow in the stark, high-altitude desert terrain, the chiseled flat-topped stone was exposed to constant peril from erosion. Production and then protection of the rock tablet was a major endeavor. Several newspapers in 1911 reported that Beatrice was working on the

**The worn inscription of the last sentence of the
Declaration of Independence.**
Courtesy of Colorado National Monument, U.S. Park Service.

engraving, but it is unknown if she really started or completed the task, or whether John was the one to do it. On January 12, 1956, reporter Al Look wrote an article in *The Daily Sentinel* titled "Local Men Find Inscription." He stated, "There is little doubt that John Otto did the carving, although no positive proof is available."

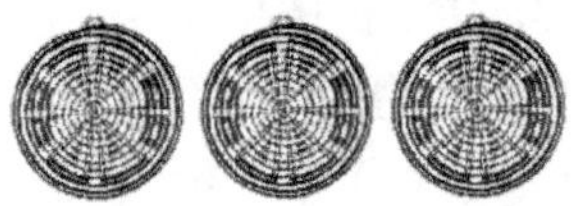

John was strongly in favor of equal rights for women and often complimented Beatrice's independence. He did not believe in traditional weddings, vows, or the exchange of rings; he believed the wedding ring symbolized bondage and obedience. To an extent, Beatrice agreed. However, as a Christian woman, she was steadfast in her desire for a religious ceremony performed by a clergyman.

She may not have gotten an engagement ring, but Beatrice appreciated Foxy the burro, her unusual engagement gift. The sturdy little companion carried her art tools and supplies for chiseling rock and painting views in the canyon during increasingly hot summer days. Foxy also provided company—standing patiently dozing or stomping to keep flies away—while Beatrice worked.

On May 26, 1911, news reports of the adventurous couple's wedding plans were less than complimentary. A headline from *The Washington Post* stated, "To Wed on Monument. Hermit of Canyon Gave Bride a Burro in Lieu of Ring." The future bride's pack burro was called "the homeliest animal in this part of the State."

The Washington Times on the same day reported, "Hermit and Artist to Wed on Mountain Peak." The writer noted, "Otto presented his intended with a donkey, which has long been known as the ugliest brute of its class in this region." Perhaps reporters in the nation's capital were unaware of the benefits and comradery of an amiable pack animal.

In the meantime, stories about the wedding ceremony were exaggerated, to the delight of readers. In Salem, Oregon, *The Capital Journal* reported on May 26, "Two Fools Are to Be Made One." The article stated that the Boston artist and the hermit of Monument Canyon planned to be married on top of Independence Rock. "For his marriage Otto is building a ladder of iron spikes. . . .The stairway is about half completed."

On the same day, *The Tacoma Times* reported, "To Be Wedded on Top of Monument." *The Steamboat Pilot* of Steamboat Springs, Colorado, reported on May 31, "Hermit Will Wed Artist in the Air: 'Hermit of Monument Canon' and Boston Sweetheart will climb to 550-foot Tower for Ceremony." The article further stated, "Both Otto and Miss Farnham are anxious to have the job completed and their only fear is that no minister can be secured who will climb with them to the top to perform the ceremony."

How the idea that the wedding ceremony would be at the summit of Independence Monument started is unknown. It could have been due to the interpretation of a casual comment, or an assumption related to Otto's attempts to ascend to the top of the tower. The story of the monument-top wedding grew, but without a specific date for the nuptials mentioned in any of the reports.

John's trails created important passages through previously inaccessible, rough canyon terrain. But Beatrice was not fond of heights. To her, the narrow rocky paths along steep mountain cliffs he had created looked dangerous and somewhat frightening. She could tolerate or avoid high trails, but a climb up Independence Monument in a wedding gown was not something she would consider.

As the wedding neared, John built his step ladder up Independence Monument. The danger of a serious fall from a rock structure more than five-hundred feet tall was real. In his May 1 engagement announcement in *The Daily Sentinel*, John had joked about the situation. He wrote, "If I fall and break my neck, the engagement is broken. BUT 'please don't anyone worry,' to place the pole and raise the flag, belongs to it, to successfully carry out the plans of our National Monument park proposition."

John climbed a bit higher each time he ascended the rocky Independence Monument. He pounded iron pipes into stone for steps and handles as he slowly made progress up the sheer rock monolith. Extended news coverage of his climb drew attention to the upcoming establishment of the new national monument.

As the month of May drew to a close, John was determined to finish pounding iron pipes into the side of the rocky cliff for the final steps to the peak. A rope ladder and sling had been installed to allow climbers to ascend the final overhang. At the top of the ladder was horizontal footing above the caprock, where the flagpole would be installed.

Beatrice watched John work from below and was observed sketching the scene. John clung to the side of the cliff—climbing, drilling, and pounding iron pipes into stone—as he advanced one step at a time. The farther he advanced up the side of Independence Monument, the less visible he was from below. As he drew closer to the top, he could barely be seen on the steep side of the looming rock cliff.

Stone formations, which surrounded Beatrice, were challenging to draw or paint. Ever-changing light and shadows required study and concentration. Her attention to detail and depth kept her mind occupied. As she kept track of John's progress from far below, she appeared unflappable as she hummed a tune and worked on sketches.

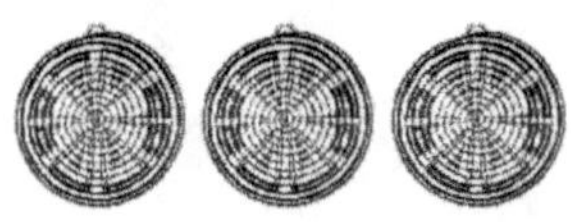

John Otto and his friend Rae Kennedy near the summit of
Independence Monument in June 1911
Courtesy of Colorado National Monument, U.S. Park Service
Whipple Chester, photographer

On June 11, 1911, a bold headline in Denver's *Rocky Mountain
Daily News* stated, "John Otto Chosen Head of New Public Reserves," referring to Colorado National Monument Park. The article indicated that appropriations from the next Congress might
include a salary for John (after five years of building trails without one) as well as money for park improvements.

The article further reported that John had completed his first ascent to the top of Independence Monument:

> It took several months to ascend the rock, which he was able to do by making a ladder of iron spikes, forced into the rock. Otto intends to plant Old Glory on the top of the big rock, when the park is formally opened on July 4, and his fiancée, Miss Beatrice Farnham, is now engaged in the laborious task of carving the Declaration of Independence upon the solid rock. This work will of itself require several months, and the presentation of the patriotic monument to the public will be the wedding gift of the pioneer trail-builder and the Boston sculptress and artist.

The article was unclear whether the installation of a flag would coincide with the newly recognized national Flag Day, which first took place on Wednesday, June 14, 1911.

John's ideas of a Fourth of July show with fireworks and a large American flag unfurled at the top of Independence Monument were close to becoming a reality. The display would celebrate the opening of the newly established Colorado National Monument and his new partnership in marriage to Beatrice Farnham.

True to his word, John and Beatrice moved forward with wedding plans once John reached the top of Independence Monument. The couple planned for their marriage to take place prior to the Fourth of July celebration. Reporters at that time pondered whether the couple was already married or not, and newspaper articles continued to suggest that the ceremony would take place at the top of Independence Monument with a crowd of hundreds of spectators in attendance.

Conjecture and rumors about the canyon wedding grew at an alarming rate. The couple's living arrangements in the canyon fueled curiosity and sold newspapers. Denver's *Rocky Mountain*

News headline June 11, 1911 asked, "Is J. Otto Married? Or is he just engaged? Questions Perturb Many." This article stirred the pot by reporting that "Miss Farnham has pitched her tent 100 feet from Otto's old camp. Neither the venturesome trail builder or the outdoor artist will give the satisfaction of settling doubt in the minds of the curious."

John claimed that he never (consciously) stated the often repeated plan to have the wedding on top of Independence Monument. In an article titled, "Makes Rope Ladder to Reach His Bride," *The Syracuse Herald* reported on May 30, 1911, "While Mr. Otto works away spiking the side of the giant stone he is a trifle dubious, he admits, as to his ability to get a clergyman who will endanger his neck by attempting to climb to the top. He has not yet requested any of the local preachers to undertake the task." If he did plan a cliff top ceremony, perhaps practicality prevailed. Beatrice, with her fear of heights, might have put her foot down in preference for solid ground, to the relief of all concerned.

"Will Wed on Monument Top," *El Paso Herald,* June 14, 1911

CHAPTER 7

The Pinnacle

Beatrice Farnham's wedding dress fluttered against her legs in the warm June breeze. A few clouds blocked the hot sun from the flat natural altar at the base of Independence Monument, about one hundred feet above the canyon floor. The bride's white satin gown, veil, and scarf were heirlooms worn by her mother and grandmother. Her attire provided a precious link to her East Coast family members, who were not present on her wedding day, Tuesday, June 20, 1911.

Never mind that the rocky uphill trail among cliffs and overhangs was a path of red, gold, and brown sandstone grit. Sandy debris on the bride's delicate white slippers could be brushed off later. Beatrice moved forward with bold strides toward the altar where she and her groom would exchange vows and begin their new life and partnership together.

Random raindrops evaporated before they hit the ground as

Beatrice looked up from the base of the looming sandstone edifice of Independence Monument. The flat cap rock atop the pinnacle resembled a sentinel's military cap. Similar cliffs and rock pedestals loomed over the canyon walls where the wedding party was convened. A dozen or so local friends, including Congregational minister Frederick A. Hatch, and his wife, Fannie, had trekked up the path to join the couple. Although Beatrice had favored a Catholic or Episcopal service, she and John had agreed that Hatch was a good choice. He and Fannie had agreed to come to the canyons from the nearby town of Fruita to perform the wedding.

John had constructed a personalized altar for their nuptials on a flat, elevated knoll. The setting was a favorite place of the couple. He was a former theology student, who considered himself an atheist. Beatrice, a freethinker, was accustomed to Sunday church services and preferred the Episcopal Church. On Sunday evenings, she and John often hiked to this special elevated rocky mound where they read the Bible or a prayer book and discussed philosophy and theology uninterrupted.

Their new partnership would be an adjustment. Both of them were accustomed to independence. John had lived alone in the canyons for the previous four years with his pack animals, a few stray dogs, and an occasional visitor. Local folks thought he was eccentric but amiable, always willing to talk about the canyons. Beatrice was a successful artist and sculptor with wealthy customers in Boston, New York, and other East Coast cities, and she had traveled and lived independently for years.

Reactions to John and Beatrice's May 1 engagement announcement had varied. *The Palisade Tribune,* located about twenty miles east of Grand Junction, was accustomed to reporting news about the local trail builder. On May 6, the paper's headline read, "Otto to Become a Benedict," which the article defined as a married man previously considered a confirmed bachelor.

In the article, Beatrice was referred to as "the artist trail girl." She was described as "six feet tall, with a free stride, straight back and shoulders and a frank, direct gaze, and speaks with slow distinctiveness of one who has been alone in the mountains' for long periods of time."

Photo of Beatrice Farnham by Frank Dean of Grand Junction, Colorado, printed in *The Rocky Mountain News* on June 21, 1911.

John was a rugged western man of the type Beatrice favored, direct and intelligent, and she relished the prospect of sharing life outdoors with him. A *Rocky Mountain News* headline on May 2, directed attention to Beatrice: "Likes Western Men. Girl to Wed Noted Trail Builder—John Otto Wins Artist—Mountaineers Despise Eastern Dolls, Says Out-of-Doors Maiden, Who Lived Among Indians." After mentioning her engagement to John, the article described Beatrice:

> Miss Farnham is in Monument park getting material for a series of paintings which she will exhibit in the East.
>
> Miss Farnham came from Boston, where she has a summer home. . . . Miss Farnham said that western men are the only real men. . . . She is six feet tall and bronzed by her outdoor work. She declares she would sooner trust herself among the Indians of the West than among the effete people of New York.

During her engagement, Beatrice shared her thoughts in correspondence with friends back east. Parts of her letters were reprinted on February 7, 1914, in *The Marshalltown Times-Republican*. She noted that she had found the "ideal of her heart, and renounced the east for all time." She was also quoted as writing to her mother: "I liked John because he is so unconventional. . . . There's no nonsense about him. He is all man."

John insisted that the wedding vow to "honor and obey" was a farce, especially the word *obey*. He removed the offending words from their ceremony, explaining his views in a June 21, 1911, *Rocky Mountain News* article: "What is the use of making women promise to honor and obey . . . when they don't have any intention of doing it. Half of the marriages performed simply force the woman to lie and I don't want my wife to make any promises she can't keep, for only so long as love lasts can marriage endure."

John shared their wedding plans with his good friend, Whipple Chester, and asked him to be best man. The twenty-three-year-old Grand Junction news reporter, cartoonist, and photographer accepted. Over the years that John had lived in Monument Park, Chester had enjoyed visiting John. He took photographs and helped with trail building, rock blasting, and constructing John's metal pipe ladder up Independence Monument.

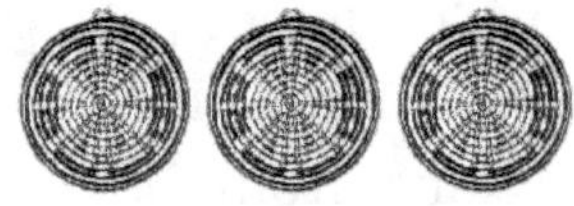

On the day of the wedding, a dozen or so invited local guests arrived in Monument Canyon on horseback and in horse-drawn buggies to witness the marriage of Beatrice and John. Guests rode a couple of miles along a winding, rocky trail. John had cleared and built the route through the rugged Monument Canyon, although guests had to walk the final portion of the trail to reach the wedding altar. Whipple Chester arrived riding his trusty bronco into the canyon, where he joined the wedding party.

Before the wedding, Beatrice prepared an impressive wedding feast for her guests. John appreciated her outdoor cooking and did not hesitate to showcase her skills. The meal, prepared over an open campfire, included a bisque-style tomato soup, roasted chicken, boiled beef tongue, salad, bread, preserves, sweets, lemonade, and coffee. Years later, in a letter to Al Look at *The Daily Sentinel*, Chester described the Ottos' wedding. He wrote that he enjoyed the "very tasty soup" so much that he later requested the recipe from newly married Mrs. Otto. Beatrice's recipe was similar to the "Mock Bisque" soup recipe published in the 1896 edition of the *Fannie Farmer Cookbook*. Ingredients for

Cream of Tomato Soup included a can of tomatoes, milk, sugar, baking soda, onion, flour, salt, pepper, and butter.

One item on the menu, beef tongue, required a boiling process similar to that used with corned beef. In 1893, when Beatrice was a teenager in Paso Robles, California, she and her parents had become dangerously ill from food poisoning after eating spoiled corned beef purchased from a local meat market. Her mother, Minerva, nearly died from the incident. According to *The Paso Robles Leader*, the family's recovery was slow.

Beatrice Farnham in her wedding clothes.
Courtesy of the Museums of Western Colorado.

The Ottos' wedding feast was a big success, without any reports of mishaps. After she finished cooking for their guests, friends helped Beatrice dress and adjust her mother's white satin heirloom wedding gown. She wore a fine lace veil, her grandmother's Japanese silk scarf as a shoulder wrap, and a bouquet of wildflowers. John wore a dark blue jacket and trousers, dark shoes, a white shirt, and dark tie. Together with their guests, they climbed to the location where John had built their wedding altar.

As dancing clouds shifted the canyon shadows, the couple stood together within the five-foot wide circle of John's hand-built altar. *The Mesa County Mail* described the wedding in a front-page article in its June 23, 1911, issue. It reported that the words *love, honor, truth,* and *justice* were spelled out on the altar with pieces of quartz within a circle of rocks with arrowheads in the corners. A mat of aromatic cedar boughs covered the sandy soil in the center of the circle where the bride and groom stood facing north and east toward the Grand River in the Grand Valley.

Photo of John Otto and Beatrice Farnham on their wedding day, June 20, 1911.
Courtesy of the Museums of Western Colorado.

In a June 21 article titled, "Artist and Hermit Marry in Colorado," *The Salt Lake City Tribune* declared, "In the wealth of eccentric detail there has probably never been such a wedding before." Adding to the unique service, John created sweet-smelling incense for his bride with burnt juniper and cedar berries sprinkled into a small fire.

Together, the couple planted a young spruce tree, "solemnly declaring that it should grow as long as their love continued." *The Mesa County Mail* from June 23, reported the planting of the tree as a "pretty incident. A tiny pine tree had been found, and right on the spot where they were made one, John and Beatrice planted this 'witness tree.'"

Although some people described the wedding as "odd" and "weird," the outdoor ceremony was traditional other than a few well-chosen word changes, such as removing "honor and obey" from the vows.

The Mesa County Mail on June 23, summarized the Ottos' marriage ceremony:

> If anyone had the notion that it was a species of vaudeville performance in which the two were engaged, a notion which silly kids of the press lent weight, they would have been greatly surprised. . . . It was different and was so intended, but nothing irreverent, outre or showy attended the ceremony. The personality of the two, is different from many. They are not queer, but independent with a deep vein of sentiment. The work which Otto has done in the Park will not be appreciated until a score of years have passed.

Later that day, Whipple Chester climbed to the top of Independence Monument and John soon followed him. Beatrice watched the men from below. At the top, John raised an American flag and set off dynamite blasts and gunfire to announce to the Grand Valley that the marriage had taken place.

Beatrice was a strong, sensible woman, unabashed by challenges, although her fear of heights held her back somewhat. If the bride and groom climbed Independence Monument together on their wedding day, or soon after for a private ceremony as some reports suggested, they did so at their own speed, without public scrutiny.

The groom dutifully applied for their Colorado marriage license, which removed any doubt that their wedding ceremony was serious and legitimate. The Marriage Record Report was filed for the wedding date of Tuesday, June 20, 1911. The Certificate of Marriage was registered and filed three days later. Beatrice Farnham was now officially Beatrice Otto, although her name was rarely attached to John's last name. However, she sometimes used her married name to avoid confusion in managing her local bank account.

After the ceremony, Mr. and Mrs. Otto returned to their respective projects. John was engrossed in modifying and perfecting his stairway to the top of Independence Rock. Beatrice planned to sketch scenes and chisel stone for the inscription of the last sentence of the Declaration of Independence. Their toil continued as if nothing had changed.

As for the bride and groom's living conditions, they no longer resided in separate tents on opposite sides of the camp. According to a letter Whipple Chester wrote journalist Al Look years later, John had told Chester, "We simply folded up one of the tents."

John and Beatrice lived together and were happy, at least for a time, among canyon shadows.

CHAPTER 8

Fanfare and a Honeymoon

Following the marriage of Mr. and Mrs. John Otto in Monument Canyon, the couple's honeymoon, a pack trip by horseback through wilderness, would have to wait. The couple planned to celebrate the Fourth of July and the establishment of the new national monument with public fanfare at Independence Monument.

The July 1, 1911, edition of *Collier's: The National Weekly* printed a full-page collage of images in a section entitled, "What the World Is Doing." The montage contained photos of the new "Monolithic National Monument Park," which was the preliminary name for the Colorado National Monument, along with separate photos of John and Beatrice.

The *Collier's* article erroneously stated, "On July 4, he [John Otto] will be married on the top of Independence Monument to Miss Beatrice Farnham of Weymouth, Massachusetts, an artist who met Otto during her travels in the West. Otto has just completed an iron ladder to the top of the shaft which is 575 feet high." By then, the couple was already married.

On June 24, 1911, *The Palisade Tribune* referred to, "Beatrice Farnham of Boston an artist of some repute and an ardent lover of outdoor life." The article attributed the wedding ceremony at lower elevation rather than at the top of Independence Monument to the choice of officiating clergyman, Reverend Hatch. But then it stated, "the sprightly couple climbed to the top of Independence rock as the first part of their honeymoon trip and will spend the remainder [of the honeymoon] among the wilds of nature, of which both bride and groom are so fond."

In his customary patriotic zeal, John celebrated Independence Day with a climb to the top of Independence Monument. Once he ascended to the capstone of the rocky spire, he hoisted an American flag on a pole he had previously installed. Once unfurled, the large American flag was visible for miles.

Four dynamite blasts echoed through the canyons, to punctuate the importance of the occasion, and to share the day with the entire Grand Valley in all four directions. In his customary fashion, the noisy salute was John's way to honor the new Colorado National Monument, Independence Day, his patriotism, and his new marriage. His first celebration atop Independence Monument for the Fourth of July in 1911 was the beginning of an annual tradition that continues today.

John had achieved several of his goals. Although he hoped for a National Park designation, thirty-two square miles of Monument Park were officially established and eventually named Colorado National Monument. He married Beatrice and accepted a position as the monument's first caretaker. Although the salary for his new job was only one dollar a month, he was able to get by and filled this position until 1927.

When the wedding ceremony was over, and Colorado National Monument was established, Beatrice now had time to consider her position, her new life, and her home among the canyons. She was married to her ideal western man and living in a scenic canyon. Production work for her paintings was set aside while chiseling words on a stone tablet was ongoing. Although the summer was beastly hot and her bank account was shrinking, she was committed to living outdoors with her trail builder husband among scenic cliffs and canyon shadows.

The mesa's high desert terrain was stark and sometimes unforgiving. As long as plenty of food and water were available, visitors could appreciate the beauty of the canyons and rock formations. Small reptiles skittered among rocks while pocket gophers dashed among sagebrush and spiky yucca plants. Rarely seen snakes, mostly harmless, avoided disruption and sought dark shadows, leaving wavy trails on sandy soil. Yellow collared lizards, handsome green reptiles with bright yellow markings, posed and watched while they absorbed sunshine on warm boulders and branches. Hawks and ravens glided on canyon breezes among cliff walls, watching below for small squirrels and varmints. The canyons that surrounded her were alive with activity.

Clear water streams flowed through Monument Canyon in springtime, but by mid-summer, they were reduced to a trickle, and they eventually became dry gulches. The confluence of the Grand and Gunnison Rivers was several miles away. July temperatures often reached well above 90 degrees Fahrenheit in the canyon. John knew the locations of underground springs and pools used for drinking water, and where to replenish water

Yellow Collared Lizard,
Colorado National Monument, July 2022

bags to carry on pack animals.

A few days after the Fourth of July display, John and Beatrice departed on their honeymoon camping trip. Pack animals carried their food, water and supplies. They rode horses and led the donkeys to higher plateaus. Their travels took them to remote areas south from the cliffs and canyons of Colorado National Monument.

Wide-open vistas beyond their usual rocky cliffs and canyons provided new landscapes with artistic appeal for Beatrice. They saw unusual formations of balanced rocks, jagged spires, and swirling, eroded patterns in sandstone. Herds of skittish deer grazed or bounded away from their approach. They followed wildlife trails that led south across Piñon Mesa.

Their trail on horseback meandered through Glade Park, on

the south side of Colorado National Monument, and across Piñon Mesa, a wilderness between Utah's boundary and the western side of Uncompahgre Plateau, south of Grand Junction.

Larkspur and bright paintbrush flowers dotted meadows surrounded by pine, scrub oak, and aspen trees. The area was lush and wild, with abundant plants and wildlife. Livestock grazed on open summer ranges, sharing space with deer, elk, and marmots sunning on rocks.

Open space provided plenty of room to wander and allowed the Ottos to relax in the peaceful quiet of their campsite without concerns about intrusive newspapers or the woes of park management. Beatrice enjoyed new views and vistas to incorporate into her artwork. At higher altitude, the clear night sky was a blanket of dazzling stars, planets, and constellations. John and Beatrice were free to enjoy the solitude and make future plans by the campfire.

Beatrice held strong views on many subjects and did not hesitate to share them. Her solo railroad travels and on-site study of Indigenous art in the Southwest had attracted national attention. John respected her independence, intelligence, and sensible outlook on many topics. These independent traits added to her appeal.

Elements of John's character attracted her as well. An article in *The Madison Daily Leader*, published in South Dakota on July 7, 1911, explained Beatrice's position. "Otto is an ordinary miner and prospector, but Miss Farnham saw in him qualities which none of her wealthy suitors in the east had displayed."

Referring to her travels to New Mexico and Arizona in the same article, Beatrice said, "There is more real manhood and womanhood among the lowest tribes of Indians in the west . . . than in the homes of the 'four hundreds' [social elite] in New York, Chicago, or any other eastern city." Although Beatrice exhibited a cynical view of her previous suitors, John seemed to fulfill her ideal.

During evenings around the campfire on their honeymoon, the Ottos could discuss goals and visions for the future without intrusion. John planned to build trails and roads to and through his beloved Colorado National Monument, to make the area more accessible to visitors.

Beatrice was absorbed in her own projects and ideas. She was concerned about her future as an artist and how to continue her business now that she lived in western Colorado. Originally, she had hoped to expand her design work by studying and interacting with artists from local Ute tribes. However, the local Tabeguache Utes had been removed from the Grand Valley in 1881. After trying to protect their homelands and tribal hunting grounds from encroaching eastern settlers, Ute tribes had been forcibly removed from western Colorado to live on a reservation in the eastern Utah desert.

Six years after the Utes' removal, in 1887, the Teller Institute in Grand Junction opened a school for Ute children. The Teller Institute was one of eight federal boarding schools in Colorado to educate (or re-educate) children from numerous tribes. Their language, customs and culture were banished in an effort to assimilate students into Anglo-American society. The Teller and similar schools were terribly managed and tragic failures, leaving a wake of a damaged culture and children in fragmented families. The Teller Institute's school was closed in 1911, the year Beatrice arrived in the Grand Valley.

Since Ute people no longer lived nearby, Beatrice could not interact with them and learn about their culture, their arts, and their crafts. Ute craftspeople, admired for fine artistic beadwork, would have been an interesting and valuable resource for an artist like Beatrice.

The Ottos' pack trip also provided an opportunity to scout for land and check routes for roadways. As caretaker of the

Colorado National Monument, John wanted to provide better access to the park for horse carriages and new automobile traffic.

John hoped to develop a road from Colorado National Monument to the town of Moab, Utah, that would intersect with roads through scenic Canyonlands National Park. A road from the National Monument through Glade Park to the Utah state line was developed. However, the route stopped abruptly at the Utah border and was never connected to Moab and other thoroughfares as John had hoped or visualized.

The Desert Land Act of 1877 encouraged settlement on arid lands in Colorado and other western states. The act allowed single individuals to homestead 320 acres. Married couples could acquire 640 acres of public land, which was previously homeland of local Ute tribes. Homesteaders were required to improve property for habitation and irrigate arid land for crops and livestock within three years. John expressed an interest in obtaining property near the Utah border.

Beatrice had told friends in the East that she and John were committed to outdoor living. She was an ardent advocate of fresh air and sunshine, and she enjoyed residing in tents, caves and teepees. However, she soon learned that dry high-altitude desert terrain could be unforgiving during hot summers and frigid winters. With John's interest in obtaining property through the Desert Land Act, Beatrice's thoughts likely turned toward a ranch house, garden, barn, and livestock for self-sufficient living near Colorado National Monument.

John had spent the years before their marriage building twelve miles of trails without compensation. He traded work for food and was grubstaked by local friends and businessmen who appreciated his efforts. The salary for his new position as caretaker for Colorado National Monument did not go far toward providing food, clothing and resources for himself and his wife.

Beatrice was often referred to in newspapers as a wealthy socialite who had acquired success with her art and designs. She came from a frugal "down east" family and had resided with her parents in a country house they had purchased outside of Boston. Her father had held sporadic jobs as a shop clerk, postmaster, and box maker in a factory.

Beatrice had relied financially on her art and design business and had previously returned to Boston with new ideas and with Native American crafts and art to sell. After her marriage to John, she planned to again take paintings back east. She needed to produce enough artwork of scenic western landscapes for a Boston gallery show. Her income from paintings would be necessary for their life in the canyons.

The upscale La Court Hotel in Grand Junction had plans to renovate and redecorate its facilities the following year, in 1912. The owners asked Beatrice to provide southwestern interior designs for the restoration project. Beatrice and John believed that if she were involved with the renovation, the design project would be lucrative.

Beatrice had additional ideas about her future. An announcement sent to newspapers, presumably by Beatrice before she left on her honeymoon, caused a wave of curiosity and speculation about a girls' colony in the new national monument.

The announcement was reported in the July 2, 1911, *Rocky Mountain News* with the headline "Mrs. Otto Bars Rats, Corsets, Booze in Society Colony—Will Spend Wealth on Back-to-Nature Community for Rich Girls in Monument Park.—CALLS HEIRESSES 'DOLLS,'" It described Beatrice's intention to organize a colony in Monument Park, called Independence Colony. There she would teach young women how to achieve independence and business skills while the girls thrived on total immersion in outdoor living.

The article explained the idea behind the colony as follows:

La Court Hotel, postcard circa 1907

Determined if wealth and work can do it, to stop the traffic in foreign titles and to prevent loveless marriages which she has seen so many of her society acquaintances contract, Mrs. Beatrice Farnham Otto . . . announced her intention today of organizing a colony in Monument park, with that end in view.

The article further explained that "Mrs. Otto declares environment has made the Eastern society girl nothing more nor less than a doll, willing to be toyed with by men of wealth, fashion and title, but absolutely incapable of assuming the responsibilities of wifehood." If John had misgivings about her ideas, he did not intervene.

While John was plotting new road construction, Beatrice was eager to take action and move forward with her plan. She felt Independence Colony would allow young women to benefit from western culture, as she had, and that frontier communities would welcome more women in their midst.

Flowering prickly pear cactus blossoms in
Colorado National Monument, June 2023

CHAPTER 9

Independence Colony

Restless reporters were eager for more details about the Ottos' future plans after their unconventional courtship and wedding. Amid the flurry of celebration surrounding Independence Day at Colorado National Monument, new newspaper headlines focused on Beatrice's plan for her Independence Colony.

Beatrice's remedy for the social ills that turned a society girl into a "doll" was park scenery and fresh air, which she felt was sufficiently exhilarating to take the place of vices adopted by bored young women. *The Rocky Mountain News* on July 2 quoted her as saying,

> We will live in the open air and recover some of the naturalness. . . . A year of life close to nature will give these girls a sane view of life, and when a real man asks the hand in marriage of a real woman, they will not be so apt to think of the luxuries which they formerly enjoyed.
>
> In our colony the use of cigarettes and of cocktails will be entirely prohibited. We expect the girls to dispense with rats

[hair fillers], corsets, powder and all of the usual accessories of our modern doll-life.

On July 7, 1911, *The Madison Daily Leader* added additional details: "The average society girl of the east, she asserts, is a 'frivolous doll' which no self-respecting westerner would marry and which no easterner with any manhood would fall in love with."

The July 2, *Rocky Mountain News*, provided more details about her colony.

Mrs. Otto will spend her own money freely to make the colony a success. She will include the girls of the "four

Photo of Beatrice Farnham Otto printed in
The San Antonio Light, June 21, 1911.

hundred" as well as the daughters of the poor, in the invitation to get back to nature.

A number of Eastern philanthropists will contribute to the support of the colony until it becomes self-supporting. The girls will live in tents, spending all their time in the mountains.

Beatrice's Independence Colony announcement appeared in newspapers while she and John were busy with preparations for the Fourth of July and their camping honeymoon. When they returned, they were met by much attention, expectation, and questions about the colony.

Some newspapers said that a retreat for young women would be difficult to establish in Colorado National Monument, which had become federal government property. Local residents were also curious about what exactly was involved in the operation of a "girls' colony" and how their community would be impacted.

"Starts Brides Farm" was the startling title in the *Washington Times*, on July 3, 1911. "Mrs. Beatrice Farnham Otto, a Boston artist, is planning to establish colonies here [Grand Junction] for Boston's slum girls, hoping eventually to marry them to Western men." The "Bride's Farm" headline fueled the rumor mill.

Four days later, an article in *The Madison Daily Leader* in South Dakota was titled "GIRL COLONY – Wealthy Lady Artist Would Educate Girls Out of Idleness". The article reported, "Mrs. Beatrice Farnham Otto, the Boston artist who was recently married on the top of Independence rock to John Otto, the hermit of Monument canon, is planning to start a colony of girls within the new government park."

The article went on to quote Beatrice:

"You can hardly blame our society girls for their tendency to becomes dolls," she explained. "They are trained to do it from babyhood if they have wealthy parents. Naturally a girl who has been used to a life of leisure and frivolity is horrified when you suggest any other mode of life, and when an honest, hard working young man asks her to become his wife she looks upon him askance unless she can be maintained in the style to which she has become accustomed."

After their honeymoon trip, John became absorbed in managing the park and tending to his trails and climbing steps. His new position at Colorado National Monument Park required additional duties, government paperwork, and reports.

During hot July days, Beatrice worked, perhaps chiseling the last sentence of the Declaration of Independence on a flat boulder, or perhaps painting. Work in the desert required an early start and then shade or shelter from the sun for midday activities. Beatrice needed food and water for her excursions. Her burro, Foxy, carried her supplies. The desert came to life in the mornings and into mid-day, when curious, colorful lizards perched atop rocks to observe her activities. As heat engulfed the morning, the day took on a sultry slow motion, with lazy buzzing bees, flies, and gnats. Swallows and ravens sailed overhead, looking for desert creatures and insects below.

Beatrice soon made plans to embark on a trip back east. She intended to visit a Boston gallery regarding her artwork and to visit her family. She would also recruit young women for Independence Colony.

Beatrice lost patience with some of the newspaper innuendoes regarding her intentions. In July 30, 1911, *The Washington Post*, quoted Beatrice as she tried to clarify her plans for Independence Colony.

We have no idea of establishing a free-love colony, as some

have suggested. Marriage today is a mockery, and not founded on love except in exceptional instances. The West is freer from loveless marriages than the East, and it is our idea to change all of this by an open-air life, which will get the poison of years of false environment out of the minds of the members of the colony.

I also intend to invite poor girls, who need Colorado climate for their health, to join the colony. It will be a mutual concern, all sharing the expense excepting, of course, those unable to do so. In those cases I shall use my own fortune to make the colony pay its way until it becomes self-supporting. Eventually there will be thousands of girls from all over the East who will be anxious to take a course in Independence Colony and as soon as the first set of my friends have become thoroughly imbued with the new idea of seeing life I shall expect them to start other colonies in different parts of the West. It might be possible to have some of these colonies in the East but I fear the contaminating influence of Eastern cities.

Beatrice's expanding plans appeared to be well under way. If her trip was a success, she would return to the Grand Valley with a dozen or so young female recruits and her dream to help young women learn to live an independent lifestyle would soon come to pass. However, the personal cost to herself was not yet apparent. A conflict in the Ottos' camp was either not acknowledged or did not exist until it was fueled by the press. Either way, only time would tell the outcome of Beatrice's steadfast purpose, to develop Independence Colony, and the couple's future.

CHAPTER 10

Back East

Beatrice Farnham Otto relaxed as she sat on a smooth, wooden bench with curved armrests in the expansive waiting room at the Grand Junction Union Depot. The bench was comfortable after months of perching on boulders in the canyons. She waited to board the eastbound train that would take her back to Boston. Several other people, waiting for the next train to arrive, sought shelter from the sun inside the station. The third week in August was the hottest week of the summer in 1911; temperatures peaked at 97 degrees Fahrenheit.

Four months had passed since Beatrice had arrived at the depot in western Colorado's Grand Valley. It was springtime then, with blooming wildflowers and sunny, mild days and cool nights. By August, canyon shadows and caves provided some relief from the heat in Monument Park, although dryness, dust, sweat, bugs, and blazing sun were a daily presence. Although John was familiar with nearby springs, his search for water for people and livestock was constant during long dry periods.

Beatrice's trip to visit her family in South Weymouth, Massachusetts was her first as a married woman. Her purpose was to visit her parents and relatives, to tend to art sales and finances, and to recruit young women to join Independence Colony. She also planned to visit Boston, New York, Providence, Rhode Island, and her former home near Augusta, Maine.

Denver's *Rocky Mountain News* covered her departure from Colorado on August 27, 1911, with the enticing headline, "Boston Artist Starts East to Get "Dolls" for Farming." The article explained:

> Mrs. Beatrice Farnham Otto, the Boston artist who was recently married to John Otto, miner and trail-builder, has gone east to secure converts to her new idea for the simple life in marriage, and expects to return within a few weeks with a dozen or more girls who will become members of the new marriage colony in Monument park.

For once, the message was straight-forward, although Beatrice probably didn't appreciate the reference to a "marriage colony."

The article continued, "Mrs. Otto has received scores of letters, many from old friends, who are anxious to try a year or two of open air life in the mountains of Colorado." In reality, the camp would be located in rocky, high desert canyons beyond the forested Rocky Mountains.

The article described how Beatrice planned to recruit interested heiresses to live outdoors "according to Western standards," to adapt to western lifestyle and to possibly meet a spouse. Considering her low regard for social courting practices in the East, she hoped recruits would be enchanted with the West and the people who lived there. She also boldly stated, "The entire American race would benefit as a result."

While she was back east, weeks turned into months. Seasons

changed. Beatrice spent Christmas in Maine with extended family members who shared her traditions and memories. Familiar people and comforts surrounded her during the 1911 holiday season. Back in Colorado, John, who was accustomed to living alone, was no doubt aware that his solitude was extended once again.

Beatrice attracted attention in a Kennebec, Maine, when the December 28, 1911, *Daily Kennebec Journal* dubbed her the "Cowgirl Artist." The article described how Beatrice presented an oil painting to her aunt, a Mrs. O. C. Webster, in Augusta, not far from her birthplace in Jefferson. The painting was a large mural of an autumn scene featuring Webster posing with her prize collie. *The Daily Kennebec Journal* described the gift, her artwork, and her background at art school in San Francisco, as well as her "winters among the Indians of the Southwest."

According to the article,

By striving to revive much of the art of the Pueblos, Navajos, . . . and Apaches, now practically lost through the influence of American commercialism, and by learning the traditions of the queer mystic designs of their blankets and pottery, Miss Farnham has created a peculiar field for her work and there is an unlimited demand for the decorative Indian Art, which she alone can supply.

Native American art was Beatrice's passion. She knew her commercial designs were dependent on Indigenous culture. Her purchase of Native artwork and crafts benefited the artisans and placed the items for resale into a new marketplace. However, Indigenous art and designs being lost due to commercialism was a disturbing thought. "Queer mystic designs," such as an ancient whirling log, a symbol for well-being and good luck, was considered sacred by Native people. The design, similar to a

**Native American pottery showing mystic designs
and symbols.**
Reprinted from Pueblo Crafts, Filter Press, 1979.

backward swastika, was misunderstood by modern European-based culture.

Beatrice's East Coast background, art school training, and design work were described in the article. However, her husband, John; her new last name; her new home in western Colorado; and her Independence Colony plans were absent. Perhaps those details did not fit into the article or were an oversight. Or perhaps her time spent in Colorado had become irrelevant. Her plans and outlook might have shifted organically when she eased back into her eastern home and lifestyle.

PART 3

I tried hard to live his way, but I could not do it,
I could not live with a man to whom even a cabin
was an encumbrance. . . . He wanted to live in tents
or without tents, outdoors.
Beatrice Farnham, circa 1912

CHAPTER 11

A Division of Trails

Beatrice Otto's trip back east stretched from a few days into weeks and then months. She and John were moving in different directions. With all the commotion about their wedding among the canyons while establishing the new Colorado National Monument, the couple apparently lacked common ground and understanding of their visions for the future. Important topics about finances, food, supplies, and shelter were not mentioned publicly.

John was eager to build new roads to make the new national monument more accessible while doing his job as caretaker and promoter. Meanwhile, Beatrice, who originally sought scenic vistas for artwork, was promoting Independence Colony, hoping to bring young women out west to learn independent living and adapt to the outdoors.

The *Rocky Mountain News* on October 12, 1911, announced, "TRAIL BUILDER NOW FARMER. Man Recently Married to Artist Will Grow Crops for Living:

John Otto . . . has taken up a piece of land in Spring Creek canon, about forty miles southwest of Fruita and announces that he will try farming for awhile, and let public work take care of itself. . . .

Otto says he and his bride cannot live on sensations, and he expects to raise crops for a living. Mrs. Otto is now in the East visiting wealthy friends, whom she is trying to interest in the proposed marriage colony, but she will return in a few days.

Unlike the Desert Land Act of 1877, the Homestead Act of 1862 allowed married individuals each to acquire two plots each of 160 acres with no cost other than filing fees. Added together, four adjacent plots per couple equaled 640 acres. John considered acquiring such acreage for farming, but then his interest in growing and irrigating crops on semi-arid homestead land apparently waivered.

On February 8, 1912, *The Daily Sentinel* published a letter from John with the headline, "John Otto Gives His Views on the Ownership of Land." He stated, "I have worked for the Monument Park proposition, that no individual should own any of it; but I am also 'working' for one hundred and sixty acres, to get a title to it from the government some day, to individually own it." Although John might have worked on some land, there is no record that a homestead claim was ever recorded. His work as custodian of Colorado National Monument drew him back to the comfort of his canyon while his wife was away.

By the following month, March 1912, Beatrice Farnham Otto had not returned. She had been absent from the Grand Valley for seven months. Frigid winter had come and gone as harsh March winds blew on the East Coast and in western Colorado.

After fielding questions about Beatrice's absence, John sent a public statement to *The Daily Sentinel.* On March 21, 1912, the newspaper printed an article titled, "The Bride of John Otto Will

Not Return to Him." A sub-heading stated, "'Our Trails Crossed; We Traveled Together for a While, and Now We Come to the Parting of the Ways. It's the Life Trail,' Says Otto."

The article described their marriage and separation: "John Otto, the trail builder, and Beatrice Farnham, whose romantic and picturesque wedding attracted far more than local attention . . . have separated. . . . The time has arrived to add another chapter to the park story on the same page—the minds of the people."

The article included a letter written by John from his East End Park Camp. In it, he repeated himself several times, as if in disbelief, stating, "She does not intend to come back." He wrote,

She (I mean Beatrice Farnham) does not intend to come back. I am kindly speaking this for her. I have never addressed her as "Mrs." . . . for a while I added my name [to]—Beatrice Farnham Otto;—but also dropped that. I did it because she is an independent girl, carrying on her own business. . . .

I believe in true equal rights. Women must have their rights and their freedom. So it is in this case: as she says she is not coming back, I must take it that way, for she is free and naturally not bound to return against her will.

In a defensive aside, John added, "Not a trial marriage was ours; no, it wasn't. . . . Let no one, however, for a moment think that I am so light and flimsy to wait years and then just marry to advertise the Monument canon."

In the same statement, John's comments also distanced him further from Beatrice's Independence Colony: "I again say, as once before, that the Girls Colony story, which was spread over the land, did not emanate from the trail camp. As she says she is not coming back, that story is killed off. Misinterpretations work harm; in this case it was an injustice."

The Independence Colony idea was finished. Beatrice's effort to recruit young women who would commit to a year of living outdoors in a remote area of western Colorado was unsuccessful. The plan failed and would not continue.

John further wrote,

The law says: one year for desertion. Before the people each one of us is single again; before the law, she is still bound; of course, I am likewise. . . . Neither one of us has any intention of going to Reno [for a quick divorce]: we will most likely seek the legal separation—for that's all there remains—in Mesa county—desertion for business reasons, with a clause put in! No sensational "divorce proceedings" in this case!— am tired of reading such.

John also wrote about his plan to find closure with his own private divorce ritual. In addition to inclusion in his statement in *The Daily Sentinel*, the idea also appeared on the front page of *The Los Angeles Times* the following day:

Every burro in the outfit, and the little dog and the two horses some day now will have a black ribbon tied around their necks, to remain there four days. Then the ribbons will be taken off and thrown into a camp fire that the wind may scatter the ashes and other ribbons will be replaced some day—the color of the Indian pinks and the wild rose. Sincerely yours, JOHN OTTO.

Whether the plan to decorate his pack animals was carried out or abandoned is unknown, but John and Beatrice Otto's marriage partnership was over. Author Alan J. Kania, in his biography of John Otto, provided details of the divorce:

At Beatrice's request, John filed for divorce. A summons was sent to Beatrice on the eighteenth day of September, 1912, stating that she has "ever since the 21st day of August, A.D. 1911, willfully deserted and absented yourself from the plaintiff, your husband, without reasonable cause." As the plaintiff, John Otto collected alimony for himself in an amount that was not to exceed the sum of $2,000 [about $65,000 in 2025].

John's work as caretaker at Colorado National Monument continued. In January 1912, he wrote a letter inviting Theodore Roosevelt to visit the new Colorado National Monument the

Newspapers across the United States featured stories about the couple's wedding and divorce. This image is from the September 20, 1913, *South Bend (Indiana) News-Times*.

following May for a celebration to dedicate the park. The letter, published in *The Daily Sentinel,* was effusive in its description of the new national monument. John mentioned that names of signers of the Declaration of Independence were to be inscribed in solid rock.

In a reply published on January 30, 1912, in *The Daily Sentinel*, Roosevelt wrote, "My Dear Mr. Otto: I wish I could accept, but it is a simple impossibility." The response of Roosevelt was disappointing, although John was accustomed to sending letters to public figures with similar results.

Beatrice's efforts to chisel a portion of the Declaration of Independence on the rock slab in the new Colorado National Monument were not sufficient to complete the task. Four-inch-tall capital letters sculpted on the rock face were never filled with concrete to provide visual contrast and to protect the text from destructive elements of nature and humanity.

Beatrice left behind another proposed project. She had agreed to re-design the interior lobby of the La Court Hotel near Grand Junction's Union Depot. The building was in the early stages of a restoration that would make it into a luxury hotel. Work requiring a designer's expertise would not be completed until the following year. Beatrice would not be present to complete the job.

The day after the Ottos were married in June 1911, *The Aspen Democrat-Times* wrote, "Miss Farnham is just as unconventional as her husband. She is a Boston product but declares that the effete East has no attraction for a woman with real blood in her veins." The article went on to quote Beatrice: "A real man cannot love an Eastern doll, and I don't blame him. The only life is life in the open and my husband and I never expect to live within an ordinary house again. We will spend our honeymoon in the mountains and then return to finish our work in the Colorado National Monument park."

However, John's ideas, including living outdoors in the canyons for several years, were beyond her limits. He had even suggested that a cave would provide adequate shelter for them during the winter. When late summer arrived in 1911 and autumn leaves fell, temperatures soon dropped below freezing on the high desert plateau. By then, Beatrice had departed.

John was pragmatic in his view of their separation as reported in Denver's *Rocky Mountain News* on March 22, 1912: "Our trails have crossed; then for a while we traveled it together until now we come to the place where our trail is divided again, she desired to travel hers separately, leaving me to travel mine separately. I mean the life trail; that's all there is to it."

Whipple Chester later mentioned a letter he received from Beatrice after she had returned back east. In it she wrote, "I tried hard to live his way, but I could not do it, I could not live with a man to whom even a cabin was an encumbrance. He wanted to live in tents or without tents, outdoors."

Burdened by sadness from a broken marriage, Beatrice had much to ponder. The love she had found with the canyon trail builder was over. Young women who previously expressed interest in the girl's colony were unwilling to commit and enroll. Her hopes and plans to live out west were failing and falling apart. Although she had often voiced her ideas and opinions, Beatrice was silent about her feelings about her broken marriage. However, her actions spoke loud and clear.

She would not return.

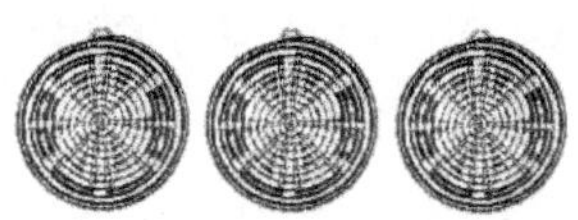

Beatrice's father, Briggs Farnham, died on April 13, 1913. At sixty-one years old, he succumbed to tuberculosis. His older brother, Charles, had also died of tuberculosis. Briggs was buried on May 3 at Lakeview Cemetery in Weymouth, Massachusetts. Beatrice's return to the East Coast from Colorado allowed her to be present during her father's final days.

After Briggs Farnham died, Beatrice continued to live with her mother, Minnie, in their Massachusetts home south of Boston. If the Farnhams were affluent aristocrats, as they were sometimes described, they did not exhibit ostentatious wealth. Beatrice's art and design work was her main source of income.

During her time in Colorado, Beatrice was far removed from art dealers, agents, and clients in Boston and New York City. Although her occupation continued to be listed as a designer in the South Weymouth City Directory, adventurous trips for inspiration in the West were no longer reported.

In spite of Beatrice's failure to establish a girl's colony, her idea received notice in Denver's *Rocky Mountain News* on April 3, 1913. Women in Grand Junction announced a plan to build a home for "fallen women" near the opening of Monument Park. The article stated, "The idea was originated two years ago by Beatrice Farnham Otto, former wife of John Otto hermit of Monument canon. Mrs. Otto planned the establishment of a home at the mouth of Monument park, four miles from Grand Junction." Women in the Grand Junction home would learn domestic skills so they could use their cooking and sewing abilities to pay expenses.

The year 1914 began with the announcement of John and Beatrice Otto's divorce on the front page of *The Grand Junction Daily Sentinel*:

John Otto, who, for over a year, has been secretly seeking a divorce from his wife, Beatrice Farnham Otto, . . . will soon receive his decree. The suit was filed in September, 1912, a short time after Mrs. Otto's departure from Grand Junction and merely charges desertion. . . .

Incompatibilities of temperament and lack of mutual understanding were the reasons, Otto said, for the separation. Since that time there have been rumors of a reconciliation but Mrs. Otto has never returned.

The fact that Otto has sued for divorce has not been known [by the public] until today. It was filed within a comparatively short time after the departure of Mrs. Otto for her eastern home. . . Now that Mrs. Otto presumably will offer no further objections to the suit and her attorney has withdrawn his appearance, the court is free to act on the case without restraint as judgment can be entered by default which is the ordinary ending of divorce suits.

The following day, January 14, 1914, Denver's *Rocky Mountain News* headline stated on page one, "Hermit and Artist Wife Part; 'Marriage Among Rocks' Failure." According to the recap, the couple originally planned to live apart for a year as an experiment. If it worked out, they would try married life again for another year, a time frame and plan that changed as the separation continued.

On February 2, 1914, *The Daily Sentinel* reported, "John Otto Granted Divorce by Judge Sullivan Saturday upon Story of Desertion by Wife." Sullivan had had earlier experiences with John. In 1908, John had appeared in the judge's court for a sanity hearing. The jury found him sane, although mentally unbalanced.

On the East Coast, *The Boston Globe* printed a headline on February 3, 1914: "Artist Bride Divorced. John Otto, Colorado Hermit, Granted a Decree Relieving Him from Bonds to Boston Girl." The same day, *The New York Evening World* printed its version of the story, which was duplicated by other papers, including *The Washington Post* with the headline "Hermit Husband

This image of Beatrice and John accompanied a January 14, 1914, *Rocky Mountain News* article.

Divorces Girl Who Chose Cave Life." This article included a picture of Beatrice with the headline "Girl Artist Who Found Hermit <u>Not Her</u> 'Type'".

Newspapers formerly charmed by the interesting couple's adventures in canyon settings now wrote flippant comments about their breakup. Another *Washinton Post* article was headlined, "John Otto Freed from Wife Famed as an Artist—Had Honeymoon in Cave." In a synopsis of the relationship, the article went on to say, "They went to housekeeping in a cute little cave at an altitude of 10,000 feet back in the Ute country, and were sure they were going to be happy ever afterward."

News of the Ottos' divorce ended the way it began, with sensational headlines and national coverage. On December 6, 1914,

December 6, 1914, *Rocky Mountain News*

Denver's *Rocky Mountain News* published a full page story with illustrations and a long headline: "The Most Romantic Honeymoon That Ever Happened—IT BEGAN with a Marriage 550 Feet in the Air, on the Top of Independence Rock, with Cowboy Accompaniment. IT SETTLED DOWN in a Cave, Because Both Bride and Bridegroom Were Tired of Houses. And THEN--IT WENT TO SMASH and Ended, After All, in Just a Plain, Ordinary Divorce."

The story began in the flowery language of the day by saying, "Another wreck has drifted into the Port of Shattered Romances, the derelict of the most adventurous craft that ever set sail on the Honeymoon Sea." The sensational article contained errors, exaggerations, and insults.

The end of the Ottos' marriage was a sad conclusion to Beatrice's life in western Colorado. *The Washington Post* article on February 7, 1914, reported that Beatrice had previously written home to her mother about John in glowing terms: "I like John because he is so unconventional. . . . There's no nonsense about him. He is all man." Although the marriage had failed, the couple refused to speak ill of each other.

Beatrice's return to the East Coast was not without scrutiny. Prior to Valentine's Day, on February 7, 1914, the *Marshalltown (Iowa) Times-Republican* reported that Beatrice's old friends spoke of her marriage as, "an oddity of a romantic girl. Tho she wrote home that she had found the ideal of her heart, and renounced the east for all time, they [the friends] are not greatly surprised that the so-called adventure has come to a premature end."

The cynical report in the *Times-Republic* concluded with Beatrice's observations:

> About a year ago, Mrs. Otto announced that she had founded an "Independence Colony," in the mountains on 640 acres she and her husband had taken up. It was to be for poor little rich girls who never had known the joys of the open. There was no instant response, and the experiment died a natural death.

John's loyalty to Beatrice was never disputed. His obsession with climbing to the top of Independence Monument was as close as he came to disengaging himself from her. The rocky edifice was always present, looming nearby, with ever-changing shadows.

After Beatrice departed the Grand Valley, John applied himself toward improving the steps he had built up Independence Monument and constructing more trails and roads to access Colorado National Monument. As he had done before his marriage, John occasionally rode his horse and led his pack burro into Grand Junction to replenish his supplies of bacon, flour, beans, and blasting powder. He continued to send and receive mail with help from friends who lived nearby.

John continued to visit the newspaper office when he was in town. His long, rambling letters and reports were sometimes considered a nuisance but always provided interesting reading, were topics of conversation, and sometimes caused a stir. His letters to the editor were read with interest by residents who followed his activities and appreciated his enthusiasm, tenacity, and integrity.

To some citizens, he was a creative genius; others questioned his mental stability. Regardless, he remained a colorful patriotic folk hero, pundit, and hermit in the canyons. He unselfishly maintained, promoted, and protected the natural wonders of the local canyons and monuments. He wrote updates about fulfilling his chores as park caretaker, trail builder, and his unending efforts as a booster of Colorado National Monument.

After Beatrice left Colorado, construction began on a new road planned by John. This winding, rocky road was called Trail of the Serpent, or Serpent's Trail. The nine-year project, which began in 1912, was a rugged trail with about fifty switchbacks. John's Serpent's Trail would eventually allow automobile traffic and more visitors to access Colorado National Monument.

A large headline in the June 14, 1912, *Grand Junction Daily*

John with his burros in the Colorado National Monument
Courtesy of the Colorado National Monument, U.S. Park Service

Sentinel said, "Flag Sent to John Otto." The U.S. General Land Office had sent a ten-by-twenty-foot American flag, requested by John, to display atop Independence Monument. The Land Office also planned to loan a team of mules with harnesses to assist John with his heavy road work in the park. John was no doubt pleased with both acquisitions. His hard work, purpose, and patriotism were recognized and affirmed.

Life continued for John with his pack animals and his dogs at his Monument Canyon camp. He immersed himself in his never-ending trail work as custodian of Colorado National Monument. John's life continued without his wife and partner, Beatrice Farnham.

Serpent's Trail, Colorado National Monument

CHAPTER 12

A Cowboy's Bride

When World War I escalated in Europe in 1914, American travelers journeyed by train and automobile to seek respite in outdoor spaces, western landscapes, and vacations in the Old West. Open prairies were increasingly encroached by new communities and miles of fence to enclose livestock. Horse-drawn carriages and wagons shared the road with automobiles.

Dude ranches were popular destinations for eastern travelers. Working ranch owners, burdened with expenses, welcomed paying guests who sought an authentic western experience. Guests at dude ranches were often invited to help with chores, ride horses, and test their rodeo skills.

Despite her short marriage and divorce in Colorado, Beatrice was not ready to give up her dream of finding her place in the West. Following her divorce from John, Beatrice again traveled by train across the western prairie. Her adventurous spirit was always uplifted by wide-open spaces as she crossed the open plains.

Sometime after her 1914 divorce, Beatrice met a cowboy

while traveling cross-country by railroad. The man was a ranch manager from Kansas named Dallas Benson. When he suggested that she visit as a guest at the ranch, she agreed. A retreat to a western ranch was exactly what Beatrice needed.

When her ability to ride horses gained attention, she was asked to perform a daring stunt called "chase for a bride," or "chasing the bride." The popular event featured a female rider pursued by a rowdy group of mounted cowboys who pretended to chase her in pursuit of a wife. It was a dramatic attention-grabbing trick popularized in Wild West shows of that time.

When Beatrice was coaxed into performing the skit on horseback, she was "rescued" from unwanted pursuers when the hero, Dallas Benson, rode his galloping horse up next to hers. She leaped onto his horse and rode away with him. The chance to perform a rodeo stunt appealed to Beatrice's sense of adventure. They practiced, performed the ride, and became riding partners.

In late March 1915, newspaper headlines again spotlighted Beatrice. On March 29, *The New Castle News* in Pennsylvania published a story with the title, "Girl Who First Wed Hermit, Now Is Bride of a Cowboy." A short, duplicated notice, distributed by United Press from New York spread to other newspapers in Indiana, Pennsylvania, New York, Alabama, Arkansas, North Carolina, and elsewhere.

The announcement stated:

Friends of Mrs. Beatrice Farnham Otto, have learned that she is married again, to Dallas Benson, a Kansas cowboy, after being divorced a year. The bride is the daughter of Mrs. Briggs Farnham of South Weymouth, Mass, and is an artist and sculptor of note.

She was married to John Otto, hermit prospector, on top of Temple Rock, 5,000 feet above the surrounding mesa in

Harrisburg (Pennsylvania) Telegraph, **April 2, 1915**

National Monument Park, Colorado, in 1911. They separated for five years, agreeing either one could obtain a divorce at the expiration of that period.

Mrs. Otto's horsemanship first attracted the attention of Benson when she performed the feat of "chasing the bride."

No details about a wedding ceremony, location, or date were published. The source of the widespread announcement was not mentioned. If the couple's nuptials took place as a staged rodeo wedding, legal registration of the alliance might have been overlooked, or bypassed.

In Colorado, *The Denver Post* reprinted an article from New York on March 28, 1915:

Mrs. Beatrice Farnham Otto, the cowgirl artist, who was married to John Otto, hermit prospector and trail maker on the tiptop of Temple Rock . . . has just announced her second marriage to Dallas Benson, a stalwart Kansas cowboy and ranch foreman. The romantic first marriage ended in divorce a year ago. . . .

Much of her work adorns the homes of millionaires in New York and Boston. . . .

Benson attracts much attention in the Boston suburb in his cowboy clothes, which he wears practically all the time, finding the ordinary business suit irksome.

Beatrice was accustomed to public scrutiny, but Dallas Benson was probably not amused.

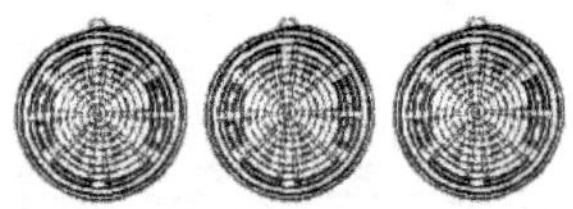

The new marriage announcement appeared almost four years after Beatrice's marriage to John Otto. When John heard that Beatrice had married a second time, to a midwestern cowboy, he held no grudge and did not speak against her.

Within a year, the marriage of the Boston Cowgirl Artist to the Kansas Rodeo Cowboy dissolved into obscurity. This time, the broken marriage, if a legal marriage had actually occurred, disappeared quietly. Beatrice's western hero and another attempt to find her place and purpose out west faded away into

Denver Post, March 28, 1915

the prairie dust of rural Kansas.

Beatrice, at age thirty-nine, was no longer a news item as an eastern artist adventurer who explored the Old West collecting Native American designs. Her partnership and marriage to the Hermit in the Canyons of western Colorado was past. Her adventures as a rodeo trick rider and second marriage to the Kansas cowboy were short-lived.

After two failed attempts to find home and happiness out west, Beatrice was again a passenger on the eastbound train to Boston. She had no siblings or offspring of her own; her mother was her closest relative, friend, and anchor. Beatrice moved back to her home in South Weymouth, to reside with Minnie. Unwanted attention from newspapers had finally ceased. The eastern artist was once again adrift to decide where her next trail would lead.

CHAPTER 13

A New Life

The world was changing. The United States declared war on Germany on April 6, 1917. America was in turmoil as young men joined the Allied forces to fight in Europe. By 1918 the suffering, destruction, carnage, and loss of life had hit home. Many surviving American soldiers were crippled, disfigured, and traumatized by battle. When they returned home in 1919, they faced disabilities, personal challenges, and uncertain futures.

By 1920, Beatrice and her mother had left Massachusetts to live in Washington, DC. Beatrice, at the age of forty-four, worked as a bookkeeper for a military intelligence office. Minnie, in her sixties, was employed as a salesclerk in a department store. Mother and daughter lived on F Street in the nation's bustling capital city and worked to make ends meet during a stressful time for themselves and their country.

Beatrice developed close ties with the Franciscan Monastery of the Holy Land in America when she lived in Washington. Their compound of buildings surrounded by lush gardens was a peaceful and inspiring retreat in the capital. Monastic guest rooms were often available for immersion in prayer and solitude.

Beatrice's humanitarian spirit came forth during the United States' involvement in World War I. After many soldiers returned home from active duty physically and mentally impaired, Beatrice started work as a lay psychologist for shell-shocked veterans. In a May 6, 1948, interview in *The Bull Mountain Bugle*, Beatrice recalled that although she lacked confidence in her skills and experience for the job, a colonel told her that nobody had experience with a war like the one then being fought. She stepped up to help veterans and tend to their needs.

After the war and her work with veterans ended, Beatrice became an advocate for woman's rights and independence. She and Minnie were still living in Washington, DC, the center of the women's suffrage movement. Women's suffrage became the law of the land with the passage of the Nineteenth Amendment in Congress on June 4, 1919, followed by ratification on August 18, 1920. It was a historic and exhilarating time.

By 1925, Beatrice and her mother left the nation's capital and purchased one hundred acres of land in the Blue Ridge Mountains in an area known as the Meadows of Dan near the town of Stuart in Patrick County, Virginia. The scenic property perched in the hills with inspiring views and vistas, was known as Lone Pine Lodge. Their residence, a converted sheep barn, was a small stone house on a hill. Beatrice and Minnie adopted a modest lifestyle unencumbered by material belongings and big city distractions.

Beatrice immersed herself in new challenges as a self-sufficient farmer in Virginia. She embraced rural life, raising live-stock and growing vegetables. Her clothing was plain and practical. Her sparse home was decorated with her artwork, murals, and sculpture. While the country struggled through the Great Depression, Beatrice and Minnie maintained their simple farm life and blended with their community.

In the 1930 U.S. Census for Patrick County, Virginia, Beatrice's age was listed as forty-five (the numbers were transposed; she was actually fifty-four), and her occupation was listed as farmer. Beatrice had finally found independence and contentment, with her days spent outdoors in the Virginia countryside.

An April 12, 1932, letter from Beatrice appeared in *The Enterprise*, Patrick County's newspaper published in the town of Stuart. She sent a proud report about her sheep herd in a letter to the editor; she was a "good booster" for Patrick County farm products and boasted about her recent success:

> I am sending you a little story about the lamb crop this spring on the mountain, at Lone Pine.
>
> One flock of 13 sheep have 23 lambs. Thirteen being an unlucky number that sounds like too many lambs—however, it figures out right. . . . (15 girls and 8 boys)—23 total and no losses—all going strong.
>
> One lamb, "Niki", Jr, seven weeks old, weighs 42 lbs.
>
> These are mountain bred, Hampshire grades, black face sheep. If any others in Patrick County have a better record for blue ribbons, let's hear about it.
>
> Faithfully yours,
>
> (Miss) B. Farnham.

Country life was physically demanding but peaceful. Beatrice applied serious effort to self-sufficiency for herself and her mother. Her clothing was plain and practical. Her flashy

Beatrice later in life, an undated drawing by Carolyn Hall.
Courtesy of Patrick County Historical Society and Museum.

southwestern attire, along with bold solo adventures and travel, were buried in her past.

While Beatrice transformed into a Virginia farmer, she embraced her Catholic religion. In Colorado, without a Catholic Church nearby, she was considered a "strict member of the Episcopal church," as stated in *The Palisade Tribune* on June 24, 1911. Similarly, she attended Mountain View United Methodist Church in Virginia because, as she explained in *The Bull Mountain Bugle*, "There were not any Catholic Churches here then and I was a person who went to church, so I went to Mountain View."

She became part of their close-knit community.

While her devotion to the Catholic Church increased as she got older, Beatrice's marriages to John Otto and Dallas Benson were slowly forgotten. Perhaps in her new life, the two alliances were disregarded, unrecognized, or forgotten.

Throughout the World War II years, Beatrice and her mother continued to live on their Virginia farm. Soon after the war ended, her mother died in her sleep, on November 17, 1946, at age ninety-three. She was buried nearby in the Mountain View Church Cemetery.

Following Minnie's death, Beatrice produced more artwork and broadened her travels. In 1948 at age seventy-two, Beatrice painted almost exclusively religious subjects. "Miss Bea," as she was known around Stuart, Virginia, had found new purpose for her artwork. She was proud that her paintings were displayed in more than a dozen places of worship.

At a 1950 Methodist Youth Meet in Ferrum, Virginia, Beatrice exhibited her reproduction of Leonardo da Vinci's *The Last Supper*. The painting was later delivered to a church in Kentucky. She appeared that year in Dexter, Maine, as a guest at a Junior Farm Bureau meeting, indicating that she was still active in farming and interacting with young people.

In 1951, Beatrice spent the summer at the home of a friend in Richmond, Maine, near her birthplace in Jefferson. She made a large, seventy-four-inch x fifty-nine-inch painting entitled *The Nativity* which was dedicated as an altar piece in St. Mathias Episcopal Church in Richmond.

Beatrice then painted a series of murals for the Rosary Portico at the Franciscan Monastery in Washington, DC. She signed many of her paintings "Fra Giacoba," the name conferred to her by the Order of Friars Minor when she became an honorary member of the Third Order of St. Francis. From there, she traveled to Beaupre, Quebec, to study a statue of St. Anne, in order

Beatrice gave this painting to the Methodist church in Stuart,
Virginia. It is now held in a private collection.
Courtesy of the Tom Beasley Collection.

to restore a similar statue for the Franciscan Monastery.

By 1951, airline travel was common, and Beatrice's world expanded. She flew to San Juan, Puerto Rico, on Pan American World Airlines from New York City's Idlewild Airport. Puerto Rico offered exotic landscapes, similar to those that enchanted her so long before, during her high school graduation trip from California to Hawaii. Throughout her travels, she studied cultural art, missions, and religious icons.

In 1953, Beatrice painted a scene of the Nativity for the First Baptist Church in Jefferson, Maine. The painting was possibly a copy of the one she had made for the Episcopal church in Richmond, where she again spent the summer with friends.

Beatrice was sidetracked in August 1955, when she broke her hip in a fall at her home in Virginia. At age seventy-nine, she spent about two weeks in Roanoke Hospital before she was released to return to her farm at Meadows of Dan.

Her physical mishap did not deter Beatrice from adventure. A year later in December 1950, Beatrice traveled on a Cabin Class passenger ship to Veracruz, Mexico, on the Gulf Coast. The winter trip provided a break from cold East Coast weather, and offered a warm climate, cultural change, and beautiful scenery. Additional journeys took Beatrice on a pilgrimage to Jerusalem in 1958, and to Genoa, Italy, in 1960 to enjoy classical art and architecture.

Beatrice's Virginia address appeared on her Social Security record in 1962. She was listed as F. Farnham, which reflected her complete birth name, Flora Beatrice Farnham.

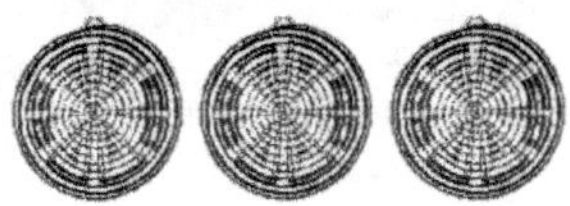

During the 1950s, when Beatrice was in her seventies, she embarked on an adventurous road trip across the United States in a trailer van with her cat. She still had the heart of an intrepid adventurer. The trip was unfettered by railroad tracks, and river routes, such as those she had navigated when she owned her boat, the *Aloha,* or railroads, such as those she had taken to study Native American art.

On her cross-country road trip, Beatrice roamed and stopped wherever she pleased with her feline friend. She exercised her independence to experience and savor views and to write notes to friends back home in Virginia. She could stop whenever she desired to enjoy landscapes, stretch, and sketch or paint.

Beatrice lived to witness immense changes in U.S. history.

She was born in America's centennial year, 1876, the year Colorado became a state, little more than a decade after the Civil War ended. Two world wars and many other armed conflicts took place during her life. She lived through depressions and epidemics. Transportation changed—from horses to railroads, automobiles, and airliners. Culture, fashion, and society changed many times, while underserved and underrepresented citizens sought freedom, equality and independence.

For her road trip, Beatrice took advantage of automobile travel to plot her own course and find her trail at her own speed across wide-open plains and prairies. So many routes were open to her. Automobiles allowed travelers the freedom to follow cross-country paved roads to seek mountain vistas and wide-open spaces. Although her route is unknown, perhaps her path took her southwest through New Mexico and Arizona to California, then to her old home in Paso Robles, California.

She might have driven on a route farther north to revisit western Colorado. Colorado National Monument was a gem to visit with the Rim Rock Road completed by the Civilian Conservation Corps in 1933. John Otto's original work had resulted in access for all tourists to enjoy, as he had envisioned.

The park had come a long way since the trail builder and the artist were married. John's first rocky trails, made passable with his hands, picks and shovels, had been converted into roads accessible to automobile traffic.

The new high road offered stunning views over Independence Monument and Monument Canyon where Beatrice had lived in a tent during the eventful summer long past, in 1911. Those memories were a mixture of excitement, love, disappointment, and heartache.

For this trip, Miss Bea was independent and could travel with her trusty cat wherever the four winds blew and the highway led her. Perhaps she chose a different path this time.

CHAPTER 14

John Otto Remembered

When the 1920 U.S. Census was published, John Otto was listed as living in the town of Grand Junction. The census was collected in January of that year, during cold winter months. At age fifty and divorced, John was one of eleven lodgers residing at a residence on Colorado Avenue near the train depot. In the 1922 city directory, he was listed as a "Trail Builder and Promoter."

By 1929, John was at odds with supervisors of Colorado National Monument regarding road construction, fence boundaries, wildlife introduction, and his on and off status as custodian of the monument, where he had toiled to build the original trails for two decades. John's work and welcome there had almost run its course. As automobile traffic increased, more people visited

Postcard showing Monument Canyon, circa 1912

the monument, exploring and enjoying the views in its formerly vacant canyons. The new Rim Rock Road was a paved thorough-fare. It had replaced John's twisty, rocky, two-and-a-half-mile Serpent's Trail with its fifty-four switchbacks. The old Serpent's Trail, which was too dangerous for automobiles and none too safe for wagons and buggies, was closed to traffic. The route later gained new life as a popular hiking trail.

John had once written, "Some folks think I'm crazy but I want to see this scenery opened up to all people." His wish came true, but not as he visualized. When traffic increased and visitors encroached on his canyon home, the time had come for him to pack up and leave.

Around 1931, John left the Grand Valley, never to return. Without public announcement, fanfare, or good-byes, he migrated back to Yreka, in Siskiyou County in northern California, where he had lived and worked in mines during his younger days. In California, he resided in a vacant post office building, which he painted brightly with red, white and blue stars and stripes of the American flag, ever true to his lifelong patriotism.

The 1950 California census listed John Otto as "Never married (single)." Neither John nor Beatrice discussed their brief marriage after they parted ways and began new lives. They respected each other's wishes for independence and privacy. Instead, they preferred to declare themselves as single on public documents.

John's reporter friend Whipple Chester and his wife, Madge, traveled from their new home in California to visit John and to talk about old times in Colorado. John also visited the Chesters in 1950. Otherwise, he lived a simple life on the West Coast, a continent away from Beatrice's East Coast farm, where she likewise pursued a peaceful and humble existence.

John Otto died near the Klamath River in Yreka on June 19, 1952. His reputation as an eccentric hermit was further perpetuated during his final years, when he lived alone. Those engaging him in conversation were rewarded with his rambling banter. Often, he spent his time panning for gold in the nearby Klamath River. He was eighty-one years old when he passed away, following a hospital stay.

In a March 21, 1955, article for *The Grand Junction Daily Sentinel,* reporter Al Look recalled memories of John. According to Look, "He was a nuisance to the newspaper people and some of his letters to the editor were difficult to understand. But nobody hated John Otto. Like Whipple Chester, I loved to be with him among the rimrocks. But never could gather enough courage to ask him about what I then thought was his unfortunate romance."

People he met in California knew John as an amiable eccentric, often rambling in his speech. He was remembered by many

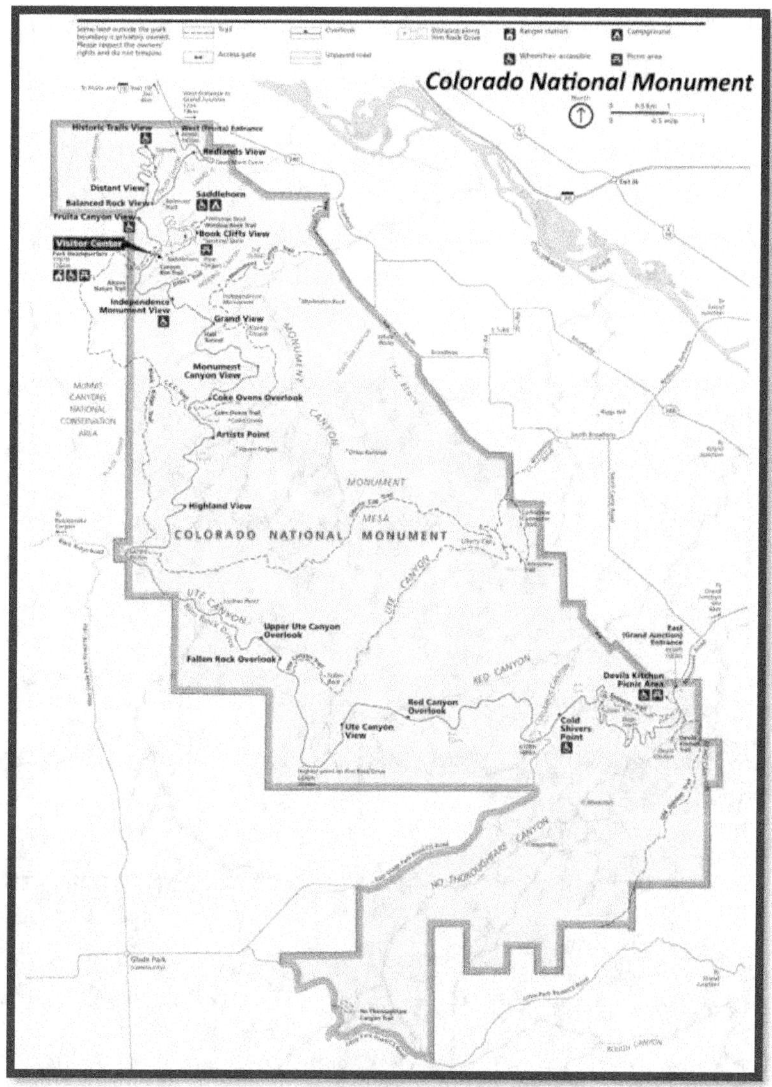

Colorado National Monument map.
Courtesy of the Colorado National Monument, U.S. Park Service.

in Colorado as the hard-working trail builder of Colorado National Monument. Many residents remembered him as a folk hero, a symbol of earnest persistence, patriotic pride, and independent pioneer spirit in the Grand Valley. His selfless work building trails gave residents and visitors access to natural beauty in the area he called "The Heart of the World" and initiated the establishment of the area as Colorado National Monument.

In Grand Junction a bronze statue, located in the 100 block of Main Street, was dedicated to John Otto in 2011. The likeness shows John sitting casually on his horse, his leg resting across the saddle horn, with his dog beside the horse. The trailblazer

Bronze statue of John Otto in Grand Junction, Colorado

looks wistfully through his spotting scope toward Colorado National Monument.

In addition to Colorado National Monument, John's legacy includes an abundance of letters and articles, often rambling and repetitive, sent to newspapers and politicians. Letter writing was his obsession. His obsessive writing habits are a colorful part of western Colorado's history that would otherwise be missing.

Visitors to Colorado National Monument can read markers that tell the story of John's time and labor dedicated to creating trails through miles of stunning rocks, cliffs and canyons. A picture of his canyon wedding with Beatrice Farnham is often on display in the Colorado National Monument Visitor Center. A bronze plaque with John's image greets visitors near the entrance.

In 2002, a dedicated group of historians from Colorado's Grand Valley commissioned and delivered a headstone for John's grave in a Yreka, California, cemetery. A granite base, quarried from Unaweep Canyon south of Grand Junction, holds a headstone with an inscription. It is a message from John Otto:

DO YOUR BEST FOR THE WEST
THE BEST FOR THE WORLD.
THE NEW DAY, GET IT GOING.
—John Otto
Dec. 30, 1870—June 19, 1952

CHAPTER 15

Her Small One Talent

Beatrice evolved into Miss Bea when she lived in Virginia during the second half century of her life. She developed sound business sense and frugal living during her years in rural Virginia. On her farm in Meadows of Dan, she found independence and the peaceful outdoor existence she sought. The farm provided a place to live with shelter from the elements, to raise crops and livestock, to enjoy community, and to maintain a simple, rustic lifestyle. Finally, she found her true home.

The path to find her place in life was long and adventurous. She loved the West for its wide-open spaces, the beauty of its landscape, and the rich culture of its Indigenous peoples. She found love with two different men who fit her wishes but not her expectations. Just as new love makes everything seem possible, lost love can cause a broken heart that takes time to mend. During her journey, Beatrice learned much about herself, although it took a toll. Fortunately, she found her true home back east, along with strong religious support, which showed her new ways to pursue a purpose for her life and her art.

Although her plans to live out west and build a girls' colony never evolved, Beatrice helped young people and supported her community by teaching Sunday school classes. Local students benefited when she discreetly helped pay for their college expenses. In her interview with *The Bull Mountain Bugle*, she said, "If anyone has talent, you just give them a little boost, and if there's anything in their head, they'll go on."

The Meadows of Dan in Virginia's Blue Ridge Mountains fulfilled Beatrice's search for a lifestyle where she was surrounded by the beauty of outdoors, which inspired her spirit and artwork. Little evidence remains of Beatrice's time spent out west. Artwork she might have produced in western Colorado is elusive. A century of extreme exposure to desert weather and natural wear has worn the surface from sandstone rocks, including the unfinished chiseled lettering.

After Beatrice left the Grand Valley, Native American artwork and her trips to the Southwest were no longer mentioned in news articles. Grand Junction's La Court Hotel was revitalized without Beatrice's help with the interior design. The hotel became a lively enterprise and gathering place for local dining and musical entertainment well into the 1960s.

Beatrice's early adventures and travels across the continent were important in her development. She loved the West and tried hard to live outdoors in the high desert with conviction and passion. When her plans did not work out, she sought a different path, which eventually led back to the East, and later to a home in the Blue Ridge Mountains of Virginia.

When Beatrice traveled abroad, she used the Monastery Pilgrimage Hall in Washington, DC, as her lodging address. In a Christmas note she sent from that address in 1966, she quoted a friend in Rome: "There is a destiny that makes us brothers. None goes his way alone. All that we send into the lives of others, comes back into our own."

Miss Farnham Celebrates 101st Birthday

Miss Beatrice Farnham, a resident of the Blue Ridge Nursing Home, celebrated her birthday at a belated party Monday afternoon. On Saturday, February 5, Miss Farnham became 101 years old.

Miss Farnham is a native of Jefferson, Maine, but came to Patrick County in the 1920's with her mother. Miss Farnham has "been all over" according to Brother Paul Trask.

Brother Paul states that he became associated with Miss Farnham through a Franciscan monastary in Washington, D.C. and has been looking out for her over the past few years.

She is a renowned church artist, whose work has hung in churches through the nation as well as in local churches. She served in military intelligence during World War I. After the war, she was a lay psychologist for shell-shocked soldiers in a veteran's hospital.

Miss Farnham was also honored as Queen of The Patrick County Fourth of July Parade.

At the birthday party Monday, Miss Farnham was treated to wine, a chocolate birthday cake, red roses, and presents as well as the presence of her friends from the nursing home and Stuart who came to help her celebrate.

Absence On Increase

Members of the birthday party toast Miss Farnham.

Mrs. Key presents Miss Farnham with a birthday present of red roses.

Beatrice's 101st birthday celebration was reported
in *The Bull Mountain Bugle* on February 9, 1977.
Courtesy of Charles Womack, Womack Publishing Company

In February 1976, Beatrice celebrated her one-hundredth birthday in Stuart, Virginia. Despite hearing loss, she was alert, in good cheer, and enjoyed the festivities, accepting the good wishes with dignity and grace. In December that year, she moved into the Blue Ridge Nursing Home after she broke her hip a second time. She lived there for three years.

On February 19, 1979, Beatrice Farnham succumbed to acute renal failure and complications of pneumonia. She died shortly after celebrating her 103rd birthday. She was buried next to her mother's grave at the Mountain View Church Cemetery, close to her farm. Her final resting place was a fitting location within the peace and harmony of her chosen home.

Flora Beatrice Farnham had no immediate family members or direct descendants. Members of her community attended the burial service, as well as members of the Franciscan Monastery from Washington, DC.

Her obituary in the February 21, 1979, *Enterprise* in Patrick County, Virginia, stated that she was a proud honorary member of the First Order of St. Francis, an honor given to her by the Custos of the Holy Land in Jerusalem. A passenger record for Tel Aviv Airline shows Beatrice was issued a visa to travel to Jerusalem in 1958, which is when she might have become a member of the order.

As an adopted member of the Franciscan Order of the Catholic Church, Beatrice hosted retreats for Franciscan friars at her Virginia farm. In June 1951, *The Martinsville Bulletin* noted a "realty transfer" of sixty acres in the Blue Ridge District from Beatrice's one-hundred-acre farm to the Holy Land Franciscan Monastery. She also donated religious artwork to the monastery, including a reproduction of *The Last Supper*.

Beatrice's close friend, Brother Paul Trask, was the informant on her death certificate, and spoke at her funeral. He said, "The material things of this life weren't that important to her . . . and [she] has donated her worldly goods to the church." Her headstone, a concrete cross, reflects her honorary membership and name in the Order of Friars Minor (OFM): "FRA Giacoba Farnham O.F.M. Died Feb. 19, 1979 Aged 103."

In reference to her art, her obituary observed, "The walls of her house at Meadows of Dan were covered with religious scenes and symbols that she sculpted and painted, such as her favorite saints, and the California missions she knew as a young girl." Scenes of the West and southwestern United States were not mentioned.

Miss Bea had written in a Christmas letter to a friend, "Makes me happy I did not bury my small 'one Talent.'" In the end, she was satisfied and at peace. She channeled her skill and effort into her artwork when she found her purpose, a home close to nature, her spiritual anchor, and a place to help young people. Most important, she found her true self.

A picture of Beatrice from her obituary, which was printed on February 21, 1979, in *The Patrick County Enterprise.*

Timeline

1870	John Otto is born in Maysville (aka Charrette), Missouri.
1876	Flora Beatrice Farnham is born in Jefferson, Lincoln County, Maine.
1881	The town of Grand Junction, Colorado is established. The Ute Tribe is forcibly removed to a reservation in eastern Utah.
1891	Beatrice Farnham's family moves from Maine to Paso Robles, California.
1896	Beatrice graduates from high school. She enrolls in the Mark Hopkins Institute of Art in San Francisco, where she lives for five years with her parents.
1904	Beatrice moves with her parents to South Weymouth, Massachusetts.
1906	John Otto arrives in Colorado with a construction crew to build a water flume.
1911	Beatrice visits John Otto in western Colorado in the spring. Newspapers report that she had visited previously and they had met in the past.
1911	May 1: John Otto announces his engagement to Beatrice Farnham.
1911	May 24: Colorado National Monument is established.
1911	June 20: John Otto and Beatrice Farnham are married at

Colorado National Monument, following a flurry of news reports.

1911   After a Fourth of July celebration at Independence Monument, John and Beatrice Otto embark on a honeymoon campout. John is hired as caretaker of Colorado National Monument with plans to build trails and roads. Beatrice plans to start a girls' colony to teach young women skills for independent living.

1911   Beatrice leaves Grand Junction on a train in late August. She travels back east to visit family and recruit young women for a girls' colony.

1912   Beatrice does not return to western Colorado. The Ottos' separation and divorce plans are announced. The girls' colony plans dissolve.

1912—1929   John Otto, caretaker of Colorado National Monument, builds trails and roads.

1913   Beatrice's father, Briggs Farnham, dies from tuberculosis at age sixty-one.

1914   Beatrice's divorce from John is finalized. On a cross-country train ride, Beatrice meets Dallas Benson, a Kansas ranch foreman.

1915   Newspapers announce that Beatrice Farnham Otto has married Dallas Benson.

1916   Newspapers report that Beatrice and Dallas Benson have divorced. She resides with her mother in South Weymouth, Massachusetts.

1920   Beatrice and her mother live in Washington, DC. Beatrice works as a national security office bookkeeper and as a counselor for disabled soldiers.

1920s   Beatrice and her mother purchase land in Virginia for a home and self-sustaining farm.

1929   The Great Depression begins. Beatrice begins working on her farm and her paintings turn to religious themes.

1929   John Otto's position at Colorado National Monument ends. He quietly leaves the Grand Valley and moves to a mining district in northern California around 1931.

1930s—1940s   Beatrice lives with her mother while farming, painting, and teaching Sunday school.

1946   Beatrice's mother, Minnie, dies in Patrick County, Virginia, at age ninety-three.

1952   John Otto dies in Yreka, California, at age eighty-one. His money does not cover the cost of a headstone.

1956—1960   Beatrice Farnham travels to Europe and Puerto Rico to study religious artwork.

1979   Beatrice Farnham dies in Patrick County, Virginia, at age 103. She is buried near her mother. A portion of her farm is donated to the Franciscan Monastery in Washington, DC.

2002   Historians in Grand Junction, Colorado, purchase a memorial headstone for John Otto. It is installed at his gravesite in Yreka, California, fifty years after his death.

2011 A fifteen-foot bronze statue of John Otto on his horse, with his dog nearby, is installed on Main Street in Grand Junction for Colorado National Monument's one-hundredth birthday. The statue is the creation of J. Michael Wilson.

Bibliography

Publications, Reports, Letters, Presentations

Becker, Cynthia S. *Chipita: Ute Peacemaker*, Palmer Lake, CO: Filter Press, 2008.

Becker, Cynthia S. and P. David Smith. *Chipita: Queen of the Utes,* Lake City, CO: Western Reflections, 2003.

Chester, Whipple. Copy of letter to Al Look, February 27, 1955, Colorado National Monument.

Colorado National Monument, Visitors Center Museum, Saddlehorn Pavilion, and National Park. Service map brochure, "John Otto's Dream," "The Heart of the World", 1907.

Fannie Farmer Cookbook, Boston, MA; Boston Cooking School, 1896 (republished).

Kania, Alan J. *Colorado National Monument,* Mount Pleasant, SC: Arcadia Publishing, 2008.

Kania, Alan J. *John Otto: Trials and Trails,* Bloomington, IN: Xlibris.com, 2008.

Kania, Alan J. *John Otto of Colorado National Monument,* Boulder, CO: R. Rinehart, Inc., 1984.

Letter to friends "Mister Fred and Lona", Jan 12, 1966, from Beatrice Farnham, Monastery Pilgrimage Hall, Washington, D.C. (PCVA).

Lohse, Joyce B. Photos, Historic Postcards Colorado National Monument, Joyce B. Lohse Collection.

Look, Al. *John Otto and the Colorado National Monument,* Dingwall, Ross-Shire, Scotland: Sandstone Publishing Co., 1962.

Mesa County Oral History Project, Interview - Lucy Ela, "Glade Park and John Otto," Jan. 1975.

Mesa County Public Library, https://mesacountylibraries.org/ program, "The Teller Institute, Grand Junction's American Indian School," Don Mackendrick, July 8, 2021.

Turnbaugh, Kay. *The Last of the Wild West Cowgirls,* Grand Rapids, MI: Perigo Press, 2009.

Newspapers and Periodicals

"A Wedding Extraordinary." *Houston (TX) Post*, June 22, 1911.

"Artist and Hermit Are Married On Mountain." *San Antonio (TX) Light*, June 21, 1911.

"Artist and Hermit Marry in Colorado." *Salt Lake City (UT) Tribune*, June 21, 1911, 2.

"Artist Bride Divorced." *Boston (MA) Globe*, February 3, 1914.

"At Altar Bride Made." *Allentown (PA) Democrat*, June 27, 1911.

"At Altar Bride Made." *Wayne County (PA) Herald*, June 23, 1911.

"Beatrice Farnham Benson." *The Evansville (IN) Daily Journal*, April 1, 1915.

"Beatrice Farnham, Noted Artist" *Albuquerque (NM) Morning Journal*, January 27, 1911.

"Beatrice Farnham's Romance at an End." *Oakland (CA) Tribune*, March 22, 1912.

Bull Mountain Bugle (Stuart, VA)

"Miss Farnham Celebrates 101 Birthday," February 7, 1977, 15.

"Miss Flora Beatrice Farnham 1876-1979." Undated.

"Cave Life Palls. Former Iowa Man Hermit in Colorado Deserted by Artist Spouse." *Marshalltown (IA) Times-Republican*, February 7, 1914.

Collier's: The National Weekly (New York)

"What the World Is Doing: Monolithic National Monument Park." July 1, 1911.

"Woman To Day – Notes of Her Activities." May 28, 1910.

Daily Kennebec (ME) Journal

"Cowgirl Artist Presents Handsome Oil Painting." December 28, 1911, 11.

"Visiting Artist Paints Scene For Church." December 25, 1951, 5.

Enterprise (Patrick Co., VA)

"Patrick Pioneers – Miss Beatrice Farnham." Jan 13, 2021.

"Patrick's Oldest Citizen Dies At 103." (obit) Feb 21, 1979.

"Productive Sheep." Apr 12, 1932.

"Ferrum Group . . . Methodist Youth Meet." *The Roanoke (VA) Times*, November 21, 1950, 27.

"Girl Colony." *The Madison (SD) Daily Leader*, July 7, 1911.

"Girl Who First Wed Hermit, Now Is Bride of a Cowboy." *The New Castle (PA) News*, March 29, 1915.

"Girl Who . . . Wed Hermit, Now Bride Of A Cowboy." *Wilmington (NC) Dispatch*, March 30, 1915, 1.

"Girl Who First Wed Hermit on Lone Rock." *The Denver (CO) Post*, March 28, 1915, 18.

Grand Junction (CO) Daily Sentinel

Ashby, Charles. "'Consistent Problem', Report details history of Indian boarding school.", Oct. 5, 2023.

"Col. Roosevelt Writes John Otto." January 30, 1912, 1.

"Deserve Aid from County." December 21, 1909, 2.

"Evergreen Spring." May 31, 1909.

"Flag Sent to John Otto." June 14, 1912, 4.

"Good Luck Spring." May 31, 1909.

"John Otto, Colorful Monument Trailblazer, Dies Unexpectedly Wednesday in California." June 22, 1952, 7.

"John Otto Granted Divorce By Judge Sullivan." February 2, 1914.

"John Otto Has Plans." June 27, 1908.

"John Otto is to Wed Well Known Artist." May 1, 1911, 4.

"John Otto Released." February 24, 1908.

"John Otto Will Get Divorce from Bride." January 13, 1914.

Little, Charles. "Beautiful Colorado Monument Keynotes Area." June 5, 1960, 36.

Look, Al. "Local Men Find Inscription John Otto." January 12, 1956, 9.

"New Depot Opens Tonight." April 17, 1906.

"Newsman Clears Up Fact, Myth on John Otto, National Monument." March 21, 1955, 6.

"Otto Receives Letter from Pres. Taft." May 27, 1909, 6.

"Otto, Trail Builder, Marries." June 24, 1911.

"Peculiar Character—Legend of John Otto." July 29, 1954, 27.

"Saved to the People." December 9, 1909, 1.

Silbernagel, Bob. "John Otto's adventurous bride sought life beyond Rock Cave." February 13, 2017.

"To Photograph the Monument." April 23, 1909.

Wright, Alice. "Epic Story of John Otto." September 15, 1957, 11.

Harrisburg Telegraph (Harrisburg, PA)

"Girl Who First Wed Hermit is Now Bride of a Cowboy." April 2, 1915, 15.

"Mrs. Beatrice Farnham Otto … Dallas Benson." April 2, 1915, 14.

"Romantic Marriage of Hermit and Sculptress." June 21, 1911.

"Hermit and Artist in Weird Wedding." *Eagle Valley (CO) Enterprise*, July 28, 1911, 2.

"Hermit And Artist In Weird Wedding," *Silverton (CO) Miner*, August 18, 1911, 5.

"Hermit And Artist In Weird Wedding. " *The Pickens (SC) Sentinel*, Univ. of South Carolina, September 28, 1911.

"Hermit Husband Divorces Girl Who Chose Cave Life." *New York (NY) City Evening World*, February 3, 1914.

"Hermit Will Wed Artist in the Air." *Steamboat (CO) Pilot*, May 31, 1911, 8.

"Honeymoon Ended." *Topeka (KS) State Journal*, March 22, 1912.

"Hotel Arrivals." *San Francisco (CA) Call*, January 1, 1902.

"If Not a Marriage." *Muskogee (OK) Daily Phoenix and Times-Democrat*, April 3, 1912.

"John Otto Dies Early Wednesday." *Siskiyou (CA) Daily News*, June 18, 1952, 1.

"John Otto obituary." *Sacramento (CA) Bee*, June 23, 1952.

"John Otto's Romance Ends When His Wife Remarries." *Montrose (CA) Daily Press*, March 30, 1915, 2.

"Junior Farm Bureau." *Bangor (ME) Daily News*, April 24, 1951.

Lindsey, Nancy. Blue Ridge Passage Resorts Newsletter, reprinted from *The Enterprise*, May 6, 1948.

"Married on the Cliff." *Avalanche-Echo* (Glenwood Springs, CO), June 22, 1911.

"Makes Rope Ladder to Reach His Bride." *Syracuse (CO) Herald-Journal*, May 30, 1911.

Martinsville (VA) Bulletin

"Beatrice Farnham." Obit, February 20, 1979, 6.

"Beatrice Farnham Returned Home." August 18, 1955, 11-A.

"Miss Beatrice Farnham . . . Broken Hip." August 8, 1955, 6.

"Realty Transfer." June 26, 1951, 8.

Martyn, Marguerite, "The More I See of Civilization the More I Like—Indians." *St. Louis (MO) Post-Dispatch*, February 26, 1911, 1.

Mesa County (CO) Mail

"A Unique Wedding.", June 23, 1911.

"John Otto to Be Wed." May 5, 1911.

"Mrs. Beatrice Farnham Benson." *Lancaster (PA) Intelligencer*, March 25, 1915, 9.

"Mrs. Beatrice Farnham Otto . . . Married to Dallas Benson." *Kingston (NY) Daily Freeman*, March 27, 1915.

"Mrs. Beatrice Farnham Otto . . . married to Dallas Benson." *Pine Bluff (AR) Daily Graphic*, March 30, 1915, 5.

"Mrs. Beatrice Farnham Otto . . . married to Dallas Benson," *The Huntington (IN) Press*, April 7, 1915, 3.

"Mrs. Beatrice Farnham Otto/Dallas Benson." *Palladium-Item* (Richmond, IN), March 30, 1915, 7.

"Noted Sculptress Marries Hermit." *Nome (AK) Daily Nugget*, June 24, 1911.

"Odd Couple and Odd Marriage Ceremony." *Aspen (CO) Democrat-Times*, June 20, 1911.

Palisade (CO) Tribune

"Otto to Become a Benedict." May 6, 1911.

"Otto, Trail Builder, Marries.", June 24, 1911, 4.

Paso Robles (CA) Leader

"A Close Call . . . Seriously Poisoned." Jan 11, 1893.

"An Air Castle." July 1, 1896, p. 1.

"B.C. Farnum Arrives." March 25, 1891, 10.

"Farnums moved to South Weymouth." July 20, 1904.

"Miss Beatrice will enter the Hopkins Art School." July 22, 1896.

"The Celebration . . . decorated parade carriage." July 7, 1897.

Rocky Mountain News (Denver, CO)

"Boston Artist Starts East to Get 'Dolls' for Farming." August 27, 1911.

"Boston Artist." August 27, 1911.

"Hermit and Artist Wife Part." January 14, 1914, 1.

"Home For Fallen Planned by Grand Junction Women." , April 3, 1913.

"Is J. Otto Married? Or Is He Just Engaged?" June 11, 1911.

"John Otto Chosen Head of New Public Reserves." June 11, 1911.

"Likes Western Men. Girl to Wed Noted Trail Builder." May 2, 1911.

"Miner Who Threatened Governor Proves to Be Harmless Crank." November 16, 1903, 7.

"The Most Romantic Honeymoon that Ever Happened" [not credible] December 6, 1914, 49.

"Mrs. Otto Bars Rats, Corsets, Booze In Society Colony." July 2, 1911.

"Otto at Liberty: First Act Was to Send an Eccentric Postal to the Governor." November 19, 1903, 16.

"Principal In Shattered Romance." August 22, 1912, , p. 5.

"Romance of Trail Shattered. Artist-Bride Too Independent." March 22, 1912, 5.

"Weird Wedding Rites Unite Trail Maker and Sculptress." June 21, 1911.

"Romantic Wedding In Monumental Park." *Journal and Tribune*, (Knoxville, TN), June 22, 1911.

Scofield, Rebecca Elena. "Riding Bareback: Rodeo Communities and the Construction of American Gender, Sexuality, and Race in the Twentieth Century." PhD diss., Harvard University, 1915.

"Silent Builder of Trails." *South Bend (IN) News-Times*, September 30, 1913, 9.

"Their Own Wedding." *Maui (HI) News*, July 1, 1911, 6.

"To Be Wedded on Top of Monument." *Tacoma (WA) Times*, May 26, 1911.

"Trial Marriage Fails." *Denver (CO) Weekly Post*, February 14, 1914.

"Trails That Once Crossed Are Now Parallel Lines." *Los Angeles (CA) Times*, March 22, 1912.

"Two Fools Are to Be Made One." *Capital Journal* (Salem, OR), May 26, 1911.

Washington Post (Washington, D.C.)

    "Colony in a Canyon." July 30, 1911.

    "Hermit Divorces Her—John Otto Freed from Wife." February 7, 1914.

    "To Wed on Monument." May 26, 1911.

    "Wed on Mountain Ledge." June 22, 1911.

Washington Times (Washington, D.C.)

    "Hermit and Artist to Wed on Mountain Peak." May 26, 1911.

    "Starts Bride Farm." July 3, 1911.

"Will Be Married on Mountain Top." *Marion (OH) Daily Star*, May 30, 1911.

"Will Wed on Mountain Top." *El Paso (TX) Herald*, June 14, 1911.

"Will Wed at Top of Unscaled Mountain." *Rock Island (IL) Argus*, June 21, 1911, 4.

"Will Wed on Mountain Top." *The Pickens (S.C.) Sentinel*, September 28, 1911.

Woytek, Steven M. "John Otto: More Than a Misunderstood Visionary." *Journal of the Western Slope* 13, no. 4, Mesa State College, (1998).

Public Records

Appointments of U.S. Postmaster, East Jefferson, Lincoln Co., ME, 1885, 1887.

Appointments of U.S. Postmasters, Briggs C. Farnum, Paso Robles, CA, 1894.

Colorado Divorce Index, 1851-, John Otto, January 31, 1914, Beatrice Jarnham Otto.

Marriage Record Report, Colorado, No. 2692, John Otto, Beatrice Farnham, June 20, 1911.

Marriage Certificate, No. 2692, Filed 23 June 1911, Fruita, Mesa County, Colorado.

U.S. Census, 1880, Charrette, Warren Co., Missouri, Emil Karl Otto, Amalie Otto and family.

U.S. Census, 1900, DuPage County, Illinois, Emil Otto, Amalia Otto, and family.

U.S. Census, 1900, San Francisco, CA, Briggs, Minnie, and Beatrice Farmem, 207 Larkin St.

U.S. Census, 1910, Orchard Mesa, CO, John Otto, 39, Guide, Mountains.

U.S. Census, 1920, F Street, Washington, D.C., F. Beatrice Farnham, 43, Minnie C. Farnham, 63.

U.S. Census, 1930, Smith River, Patrick, VA, Beatis F. Farnham, 45, Minnie C. Farnham, 75.

U.S. Census, 1940, Blue Ridge, Patrick, VA, Beatrice Farnham, 64, Minnie C. Farnham, 86.

U.S. Census, 1950, Oak Bar, Siskiyou, CA, John Otto, 79, Never Married (single).

U.S. Civil Service, Clerks/Post Office, Miss F.B. Farnum, 19, Paso Robles, CA, 1895.

U.S. City Directories, 1900, 1901, San Francisco, CA, Miss F. Beatrice, and Briggs C. Farnum.

U.S. City Directory, South Weymouth, MA, 1910-11.

U.S. City Directory, Grand Junction, CO, 1911.

U.S. Certificate of Death, S. Weymouth, Massachusetts, Briggs Carter Farnham, April 30, 1913.

U.S. Certificate of Death, Meadows of Dan, Virginia, Minerva C. Farnham, Nov 17, 1946.

U.S. Certificate of Death, Stuart, Virginia, Beatrice (NMN) Farnham, February 19, 1979.

U.S. Death Record - Beatrice Farnham - b. Feb 19, 1979, d. Feb. 5, 1876, Patrick Co., VA

U.S. Passenger List - Puerto Rico, Beatrice Farnham - Franciscan Seminary, July 22, 1951.

U.S. Passenger List - Vera Cruz, Beatrice Farnham - Franciscan Monastery, December 4, 1956.

U.S. Passenger List - Israel Jerusalem, F Beatrice Farnham - Franciscan Seminary, May 7, 1958.

U.S. Passenger List - EL AL Airline - from Tel Aviv, F Beatrice Farnham (82) – May 7 1958.

U.S. Passenger List - Genoa, Beatrice F. Farnham - Franciscan Seminary, May 21, 1960.

U.S. Social Security Death Index, F. Farnham, Patrick Co., VA., Issue 1962, Death Feb 1979.

U.S. Voter Registration, 1900, San Francisco, CA, Briggs C. Farnum, 207 Larkin St.

Internet Resources

Albuquerque. "Stunning Alvarado Hotel," https://albuquerque.com/the-fantastic-alvarado-hotel/.

Ancestry.com (subscription), https://www.ancestry.com/

Colorado Business Directory, 1911 Grand Junction, Mesa County, https://files.usgwarchives.net/.

California Historical Marker, Site of the Mark Hopkins Institute of Art, No. 754, Erected 1961, Historical Marker Database: https://www.hmdb.org/m.asp?m=143440.

Colorado Historic Newspapers, https://www.coloradohistoric-newspapers.org/.

Colorado National Monument,
    https://www.nps.gov/colm/planyourvisit/basicinfo.htm/
Extreme Weather Watch, https://www.extremeweather-
    watch.com/cities/grand-junction/year-1911.
Find-A-Grave, https://www.findagrave.com/
    Beatrice Farnham, b. 5 Feb 1876, d. 19 Feb 1979, Mountain
    View United Methodist Church Cemetery, Meadows of Dan,
    Patrick Co., VA.
    John Otto, b. 30 Dec 1870, d. 19 Jun 1952, Evergreen Cemetery,
    Yreka, CA.
Franciscan Monastery of the Holy Land in America
    https://www.google.com/search?client=firefox-b-1-d&q=Fran-
    ciscan+Monastery+of+the+Holy+Land+in+America.
Grand Junction Union Depot, https://www.gjuniondepot.com/the-
    history/.
Historical Marker Database, "Site of the Mark Hopkins Institute of
    Art," https://www.hmdb.org/m.asp?m=143440.
Historical Photos of Fruita, https://www.facebook.com/Histori-
    calFruitaPhotos.
History Colorado, "Homestead Act" article, 2020, ColoradoEncy-
    clopedia.org/article/homestead.
Lower Valley Heritage Room, Fruita, CO, https://www.face-
    book.com/TheLVHR/.
Mesa County Oral History Project, https://mesacountylibrar-
    ies.org/mcohp/.
Mesa County Public Library, https://mesacountylibraries.org/.
Minor, Will C., "The Year In Pinon Mesa," from *Footprints On The
    Trail*, Historical Museum and Institute of Western Colorado,
    1950, https://glade-park.com/pinon-mesa-a-year-on.html.
Museums of Western Colorado, https://museumsofwest-
    ernco.com.
National Archives.gov, "Declaration of Independence: A Tran-
    scription", www.archives.gov.
National Park Service, https://www.nps.gov/.
National Park Service, *Colorado National Monument,* "John Otto,"

https://www.nps.gov/colm/learn/historyculture/john-otto.htm.

Paso Robles, CA Area Historical Museum, https://www.paso-robleshistorymuseum.org/.

Patrick County, VA Historical Museum, https://patcovahistory.org/.

"Pueblos of New Mexico," https://santodomingopueblo.com/our-history/.

United Church of Christ, "The Challenge of Modern Biblical Scholarship", Karl Emil Otto, by Scott Hall, https://www.ucc.org/ucc_roots_may_2017/.

U-S-History.com/pages/h2716html – historical article, San Francisco Art Institute and Mark.

Ute Indian Tribe of the Uintah Ouray Reservation, https://indian.utah.gov/ute-indian-tribe-of-the-uintah-ouray-reservation/.

Virginia Chronicle Library of Virginia, www.virginiachronicle.com.

Marriage Notices

Mrs. Beatrice Farnham Otto To Dallas Benson in 1915:
The Evansville (IN) Daily Journal, April 1, 1915, 4.
Harrisburg (PA) Telegraph, April 2, 1915, 14.
The Huntington (IN) Press, April 7, 1915, 3.
Kingston (NY) Daily Freeman, March 27, 1915.
Lancaster (PA) Intelligencer, March 25, 1915, 9.
Montgomery (AL) Times, March 29, 1915, 2.
New Castle (PA) News, March 29, 1915.
Palladium-Item, (Richmond, IN), March 30, 1915, 7.
Pine Bluff (AR) Daily Graphic, March 30, 1915, 5.
Wilmington (NC) Dispatch, March 30, 1915, 1.

Article Sources, Ancestry.com, Colorado Historic Newspapers.com, Newspapers.com, Library of Congress LOC.gov, Mesa County Libraries (microfilm), Grand Junction, CO.

Acknowledgments

While I searched for Beatrice Farnham's story among canyon shadows, I encountered many fine people along the path. Colorado National Monument Association offered opportunities to explore the canyons from many perspectives. I hiked through terrain where Trail Builder John Otto and Eastern Artist Beatrice Farnham lived during the eventful summer of 1911. I attended art classes in the park, which introduced me to joys of outdoor sketching and difficulties of painting views of rocky landscapes.

National Park Service employees, rangers, caretakers, and association employees share the wonders of Colorado National Monument with visitors from all walks of life. Ongoing thanks go to the rangers and support personnel, including Mikki Murray, Rachel Berger, Kait Thomas, and Sharon Dixon, who continually share valuable assistance and information.

Mesa County Public Library in Grand Junction is a gem of information, resources, and history programs in conjunction with Mesa County Historical Society. I am grateful for assistance with materials, ideas, and resources from history and research librarians at Mesa County's Main Library, especially for the help from Ike Rakiecki, librarian, artist and hiker.

Paso Robles Historical Society in southern California provided information about Beatrice Farnham's high school years on the West Coast. Thanks to researcher Patty Breckow, who located and shared great articles.

The Patrick County Historical Society and Museum filled in information about the later portion of Beatrice's long life. Contacts and encouraging responses from support personnel and research assistants, especially Greg Arens, Larry Hopkins, and John Reynolds, confirmed that I was onto a great story and I should continue. They were especially helpful with providing information that filled in gaps and providing pictures.

Support and encouragement from friends and peers in

Women Writing the West and Western Writers of America are priceless. Hearty thanks to John Nesbitt, western writer, instructor, and author of *Shaping the Story*, who generously assisted me as I struggled with the story's shape and path.

I am deeply grateful to Filter Press publisher Julie Van-Laanen, who embraced the story of Beatrice Farnham with enthusiasm and expertise, and directed it to fruition. Filter Press's high standards and integrity flourish with her skills and insight. I also appreciate previous Filter Press publisher, Doris Baker, for her continued interest and assistance as a reader of my latest work.

My friends, family, and especially my husband, Don, provide precious support, while wondering where my trail will lead. I hope readers enjoy Beatrice Farnham's story and the shifting trails she chose, which sent her on a wild ride through western Colorado.

Appendix
Tomato Bisque Soup Recipe
From the 1896 *Fannie Farmer Cookbook*

1 can of tomatoes
2 teaspoons sugar
1 pint water
1 teaspoon salt
12 peppercorns
1/8 teaspoons soda
Bit of bay leaf
2 tablespoons butter
4 cloves
3 tablespoons flour
1 slice onion
[milk added for bisque]

Cook the first six ingredients
Twenty minutes; strain, add salt
And soda; bind, and strain into tureen.

John Otto & Beatrice Farnham Wedding Meal
   "Miss Farnham had prepared:
      Roast Chicken
      Boiled Tongue
      Exquisite Salad
      Tomato Bisque
      All over an open fire
   And Sweets and Preserves
   … it was feast to stir jaded palates."

From: *Mesa (CO) County Mail*, June 23, 1911.

About the Author

Joyce B. Lohse, Western History Journalist and Author

Colorado journalist and author, Joyce B. Lohse, combines research and western history with writing articles and award-winning books for all ages. Her seven previous Filter Press books include four titles in the "Now You Know Bio" series. She has five awards from the Colorado Independent Publishers Association, and a Colorado Authors' League's Top Hand Award. She is also a two-time finalist for the Women Writing the West WILLA Literary Award. Her writings are included in Pikes Peak Library District regional history collections, and her 2025 short story was chosen for inclusion in *She Rode West* from Saddlebag Dispatches. Joyce is a member of Western Writers of America, Women Writing the West, and Denver Woman's Press Club. Currently, she is searching for stories among rocky canyons in western Colorado.

Other Books by Joyce B. Lohse

Spencer Penrose: Builder and Benefactor, — Filter Press, 2016, ISBN: 13-978-86541-190-6.

Baby Doe Tabor: Matchless Silver Queen, — Filter Press, 2011, ISBN: 978-0-86541-107-4.

General William Palmer: Railroad Pioneer, — Filter Press, 2009, ISBN: 978-0-86541-092-3.

Unsinkable: The Molly Brown Story, — Filter Press, 2006, ISBN: 0-86541-081-X.

Emily Griffith: Opportunity's Teacher, — Filter Press, 2005, ISBN: 0-86541-077-1.

Justina Ford: Medical Pioneer, — Filter Press, 2004, ISBN: 0-86541-074-7.

First Governor, First Lady: John & Eliza Routt of Colorado, — Filter Press, 2002, ISBN: 0-86541-063-1.

A Yellowstone Savage: Life in Nature's Wonderland, — J. D. Charles Publishing, 1988, ISBN: 978-0944915-004.

Books by Joyce B. Lohse are available from local booksellers, FilterPressBooks.com, and Amazon.com.